The Pearl of Great Price

*The True Story of One Man's Quest
For the Most Precious Treasure in the World*

Orest Stocco

The Pearl of Great Price

Copyright © 2015 by Orest Stocco

All rights reserved. No part of this book may be reproduced or transmitted in any form or by any means without written permission of the author.

ISBN 978-1-926442-04-4

Edited by Penny Lynn Cates

Cover Design by Penny Lynn Cates

ALSO BY OREST STOCCO

NOVELS

The Golden Seed
Tea with Grace
Jesus Wears Dockers
Healing with Padre Pio
Keeper of the Flame
My Unborn Child
On the Wings of Habitat
What Would I Say Today If I Were to Die Tomorrow?

NON FICTION

The Lion that Swallowed Hemingway
The Sum of All Spiritual Paths
Do We Have An Immortal Soul?
Stupidity Is Not a Gift of God
Letters to Padre Pio
Old Whore Life
Just Going with the Flow
Why Bother? The Riddle of the Good Samaritan

*Alice, for your love, your courage, and your grace,
I dedicate this book to you.*

"The truth is that no matter where I went,
I was always looking for myself."

Shirley MacLaine

A WORD FOR THE READER

I didn't want to write this story, and I kept putting it off for months; but it kept nagging at me until I wrote a spiritual musing for my blog titled "The Pearl of Great Price" just to get my Muse off my back.

But that didn't work, and out of respect for my Muse—which has a tendency to dry up my well of creative energy when I don't write what I've been called upon to write—I decided to tell the story of what Joseph Campbell called the hero's journey.

Of all my books, this was the hardest one to write; not because I don't trust my Muse, I certainly do, but because I knew how personal it would have to be, and my greatest fear as a writer has always been to write about my private life, which was completely ludicrous given that all of my books are so intensely autobiographical; but telling the unbelievable story of how I found *the pearl of great price* terrified me, and the reader has a right to know why.

Let's say that a certain scientifically mystifying *élan vital* runs through life like a powerful current of electric energy runs through hydro lines, and let's further say that creative writers tap into this vital force of life when they write about the human condition; but just as one would get a terrible shock by grabbing an exposed hydro line, so too will a writer shock himself when he taps into the energy of his most private and personal experiences, which is why writers write fiction to buffer the shock of their most private life, like Philip Roth did when he wrote about masturbation in his novel *Portnoy's Complaint* that launched his literary career, and the same with John Updike when he wrote his breakaway novel *Couples* that was all about adultery.

But my private life was much more personal than masturbation and adultery, neither of which were unfamiliar to me; it was about the quest for my lost soul, a subject so intimate and personal that even my most valiant hero Carl Gustav Jung dared not publish the fantastic story of his own incredible quest for his lost soul during his lifetime for fear of the shock to his life; but fifty years after his death his family finally gave permission to have the chronicle of his "confrontation with the unconscious" known as *The Red Book* released to a grateful public.

The hero's journey is a sacred journey, and not everyone is called to go on the hero's journey; only those souls that have come to the end of the line and have nowhere else to go. Scared and alone, they have only one road left open to them, and they go on the hero's journey to find their lost soul.

I found my lost soul, and I was called upon to tell my incredible story. I knew that if I refused to heed the call I would suffer the unbearable guilt of not being true to myself, which was sure to make my life miserable; and so, as the old proverb goes, I did what I had to do and let the Devil take the hindmost. And as improbable as it may appear to be, it's all true; and I hope you like my story.

Orest Stocco,
Georgian Bay, Canada
February 9, 2015

Table of Contents

1. *The Inspiration for my Story* 1
2. *Sage Advice from Shirley MacLaine* 5
3. *Feasting on the Now* 10
4. *The Roses and the Thorns* 15
5. *Life is Pretty Much Happenstance* 20
6. *The Tragedy of Effort* 26
7. *Drawing the Line* 32
8. *When Life Is Not Enough* 37
9. *"Creation's Giddy Bliss"* 41
10. *The Divine Plan of God* 47
11. *The Way of Being and Non-being* 51
12. *The Lure of Our Becoming* 55
13. *Life Is Not a Useless Passion* 59
14. *Our Two Destinies* 64
15. *Bridging the Great Divide* 68
16. *Follow Life and the Living* 72
17. *The Wonder of Story* 76
18. *The Dust on a Butterfly's Wings* 79
19. *When the Two Become One* 82

20. *The Surrendering Heart* 87

21. *Unfinished Novel* 91

22. *The Endstory* 94

23. *Alice's Unspeakable Secret* 100

24. *Letter to Alice* 104

25. *The Holy Fire of God* 110

26. *Honoring Alice's Choice* 114

27. *Confirmation* 126

Afterward 128

1. *The Inspiration for my Story*

Every person has their own story, and every story is unique in the sacred drama of life's divine mystery; but regardless how distinctive our stories may be, we are all driven to become who we are meant to be, and this makes us all the same.

"The privilege of a lifetime is to be who you are," said Joseph Campbell, who discovered the archetypal pattern of the hero's journey in all the great mythologies of the world; but not until one is called to be who they are meant to be will they be pulled into the sacred currents of the hero's journey.

I heard the call in high school. Perhaps in elementary school with my desire to become a writer. The call was faint, but in high school I read *The Razor's Edge* by Somerset Maugham and wanted to go to France like my hero Larry Darrel; but not until the cruel forces of fate severed me from my life six years later did I get swept away by the unyielding currents of the hero's journey, and I sailed from New York City on an ocean liner to France to begin my quest for my true self.

The hero's journey is man's quest for his lost soul, the most precious treasure in the world, which has been told in all the great literature of the world—Dante's *Divine Comedy;* Bunyan's *Pilgrim's Progress*; the anonymous play *Everyman;* the Sufi allegory *The Conference of the Birds*; and the modern novel *The Alchemist* by Paulo Coelho, to name the most obvious. But the story that captured my heart more than any other was C. G. Jung's unbelievable quest for his lost soul, which he recorded in his journals and released to the world as *The Red Book* fifty years after his death because Jung did not want it published in his lifetime.

At the age of forty, Jung had achieved everything that he had wished for in his life, "honor, power, wealth, knowledge, and every human happiness," but then the desire for an increase in all of these "trappings" ceased, and horror came over him.

"My soul, where are you?" asked Jung, in frozen terror; and thus began his descent into the terrifying depths of his unconscious to search for the soul he had forfeited for the enviable success of his life. This was the heroic journey that defined his remarkable life.

Carl Gustav Jung became my personal hero, and from him I learned the sacred meaning of story, which was confirmed by his friend in Laurens van der Post's memoir *Jung and the Story of Our Time*: In the Bergholzli psychiatric hospital in Zürich, Jung learned from his patients that story was the personality's most precious possession, whether one knew it or not; and when one's story was interrupted by whatever traumatic experience (shocking betrayal, the death of a child, bankruptcy, whatever), it threw one's mind into confusion; and with studious patience and compassion Jung came to see that the only way to cure his mental patients was to reconnect them with their life story. This was Jung's greatest discovery, and the reason he went on the hero's journey to reconnect with the interrupted story of his own life.

"Story was the seed and essence of their history," Laurens van der Post learned from an old Bushman grandmother, who refused to let the young boy hear her stories with the Bushman children because he had not learned to respect the sacred mystery of the Bushman's mythology; and Laurens van der Post came to realize that "without a story of its own no culture, society, or personality could survive," because **story is the bearer of the meaning and purpose of life,** the ultimate purpose being, as I painfully came to learn from my own heroic journey, the quest for one's true self—what Jesus, the greatest storyteller of all, called *"the pearl of great price."*

"Again, the kingdom of heaven is like unto a merchant man, seeking goodly pearls: Who, when he had found one pearl of great price, went and sold all that he had, and bought it," said Jesus in his most sacred parable.

Who is the *merchant man,* and why did Jesus liken him unto *the kingdom of heaven*? Why is he seeking *goodly pearls*? What does Jesus mean by *kingdom of heaven*? And what is *the pearl of great price*? This is the elusive, comprehensive mystery of story.

Jesus said to his disciples that it was not given to the public to know the mysteries of *the kingdom of heaven,* but to them it was; and in private he revealed the sacred mystery of his parables. *"For whosoever hath, to him shall be given, and he shall have more abundance; but whosoever hath not, from him shall be taken away even that he hath,"* said Jesus to his disciples.

I had to "work" on myself with relentless commitment with Gurdjieff's teaching to initiate myself into the secret way of life that Jesus revealed to his disciples in private, and I finally broke the code of Christ's cryptic sayings; and now I am called to take the logic of Christ's teaching to its conclusion and reveal the mysterious truth of *the pearl of great price*. But I cannot do this without explaining what Jesus meant when he said that his disciples were ready for the secret knowledge of *the kingdom of heaven* while the public at large was not; and so one may well ask, what made his disciples ready?

It took most of my life to answer this question, which I've written about in my little book *Do We Have an Immortal Soul?* and need not expound upon here; so suffice to say that my initiation into the mysteries of life allowed me to see that we are all sparks of divine consciousness whose purpose in life is to grow in our own identity until we are called back home to God, which is what Jesus meant by his saying *"Many are called, but few are chosen"* and which I expound upon in *Why Bother? The Riddle of the Good Samaritan*, a travelling companion to my novel *Healing with Padre Pio*; and it is here that I have a parting of the ways in my gnostic understanding of Christ's most sacred parable, *the parable of the pearl of great price*.

There is such exquisite irony in this parable that I don't know if I can do it justice, but I must try for the sake of my story; because in this irony can be seen the infinite mercy of God's love and the unbelievable depths of man's vanity, an irony that I would have remained oblivious to had I not bottomed out of my own vanity in my spiritual healing experience with the Ascended Master that inspired my novel *Healing with Padre Pio*; but just what is this exquisite irony in the parable of *the pearl of great price* that puts a frown upon the face of man's recalcitrant spiritual ignorance.

In a word, when all is said and done the secret of Christ's teaching—that part of his teaching that he could not give to the public because the public was not ready to receive it—is not a secret at all; it is there for everyone to see, if they have "eyes" to see and "ears" to hear, that is. And that's the mystery that took the best part of my life to resolve and now sets me apart from the rest of the world.

I went through many teachings and more suffering than I care to remember to arrive at the simple truth that the great secret of life is that there is no secret teaching because life itself is the way to our divine nature, and it took many years to get over my anger at the world for playing me for an arrogant fool (hence my inspiration for writing *Old Whore Life, Exploring the Shadow Side of Karma*); but now I'm free to look at life unobfuscated by the spiritually stupefying vanity of humanity, and I can tell the story of my own heroic quest for my true self in the dark corners of my own unconscious.

Every teaching claims its own truth—Christianity's paralyzing fear that only through Jesus Christ can we be saved from eternal damnation; Gurdjieff's terrorizing premise that we are not born with an immortal soul and must create our own soul with conscious effort; Buddhism's disconcerting belief that our autonomous and individual self is ephemeral and unreal; the New Age Religion of the Light and Sound of God's vaunting avowal of being the most direct path to God with its tacit claim to the Inner Master, and which I lived for over thirty years; the dangerous teaching of an offshoot Christian solar cult that purports the rays of the sun to be imbued with the sacred Logos, which did irreparable damage to my eyesight; the ancient shamanic ways of dream travel brought to the modern world by "dream archeologist" Robert Moss; the spirited modern mystic Caroline Myss's spiritually inspired teachings of entering the sacred castle of our soul for spiritual growth and healing; Mystery School founder Dr. Jean Houston's *enlightened attitude* on life and the human potential movement; Deepak Chopra and the future of God; Jungian shadow-work to integrate our divided self; and, of course, material science's pathology of non-belief in God, soul, and the afterlife, and on and on; but when all is said and done, all ways lead to *the pearl of great price*, which is the key to *the kingdom of heaven*. In short, every path in life leads to our true self; and the more true we are to our own self, the more we realize our divine nature. That's the exquisite irony of Christ's most sacred parable, and the inspiration for my story…

2. Sage Advice from Shirley MacLaine

"What is it you feel now, or do you feel now a sense of, not urgency, but what you would most want people to know?" Oprah Winfrey asked Shirley MacLaine, a lifelong seeker on the cusp of eighty talking about her new book *What If*...and MacLaine's response confirmed what every seeker who has made a connection with their inner self learns about the secret way of life: *"The notion that all you really need in life is some fresh water, a good hat, and a really good pair of shoes."*

Shirley laughed when she said this, and so did Oprah and her *Super Soul Sunday* studio audience; but they didn't grasp the profound depths of Shirley MacLaine's soul-scoured wisdom, because in her answer can be found the secret of Christ's most sacred parable—*the parable of the pearl of great price.*

The pearl of great price is our true self, the divine essence of our being; and Shirley MacLaine's response addressed her life-long quest for her true self dressed up in the metaphor of her Santiago de Compostela pilgrimage that she wrote about in *The Camino,* a metaphor that distills all her years of self-questing into a pithy little notion that made Oprah and her audience laugh. But the irony is that it wasn't meant to be funny at all. It was meant to reveal the simple truth that we have to discard all the "baggage" of our life to find our true self, just as the sixty year old Shirley MacLaine had to discard everything that weighed her down and didn't need to complete her pilgrimage on the lonely road to Santiago de Compostela.

There is so much life wisdom presupposed in MacLaine's pithy little notion that I don't know where to begin; but to tell the story of my search for my true self I have to begin at the beginning, and the beginning was my past-life regression to the Body of God where all new souls come from. But to tell this part of my story, I have to beg the reader's humble indulgence…

Truth seeking is not for everyone; and yet, paradoxically, we are all on the same never-ending road to truth because, as Jesus said to Glenda Green in *The Keys of Jeshua*, "*There is nothing but the self and God.*" If this is so, which I confirmed with my own journey of self-discovery, then the truth that every seeker is looking for is the truth of their own divine nature; and herein lies the quandary, because to find our true self we have to *become* our true self, which is the essential purpose of all life. This is why our greatest need in life is not for the air we breathe, the water and food we need to survive, or sex even; but the need to be who we are meant to be, just as the acorn seed's greatest need is to *become* an oak tree—an *a priori* teleological need which is served by all of our other needs.

As simple as this may be, my greatest need in life was to be myself, just as Shirley MacLaine's greatest need was to be herself. That's why she said in *I'm Over All That* that no matter where she went she was always looking for herself; which puts a whole new spin on the concepts of karma and reincarnation, because without karma and reincarnation we cannot *become* our true self.

This is a big mouthful, and completely indigestible for the non-believer; and yet, the further down the road one travels in their unconsciously driven need for their true self, the more the secret way of life will reveal itself to them until one day karma and reincarnation no longer become a matter of the mind, but a personal gnostic truth. This is why there is only self-initiation into the mysteries of life.

Karma and reincarnation are no longer concepts for me, then; they exist as spiritual laws that govern one aspect of soul's evolution through life (there are other aspects, as I came to learn), and by soul I mean the seed of our divine nature. Which brings me back to my past-life regression to the Body of God where all souls come from and where we must return because it is written in the Divine Plan of God that I expounded upon in my novel *Cathedral of My Past Lives*. How many books and teachings I had to puzzle my way through to awaken to the Holy Cathedral of God's Divine Plan, I cannot say; but had it not been for the omniscient guiding force of life, I would never have solved the riddle of *the pearl of great price*; and it all started with a coincidental meeting with a past-life regressionist when Penny and I relocated to beautiful Georgian Bay, South Central Ontario…

Many years ago in the early stages of my quest for my true self, I read Jess Stearn's *Edgar Cayce: The Sleeping Prophet*, which prompted me to read his book *The Search for the Soul: Psychic Lives of Taylor Caldwell*; and as I read this mind-expanding book I knew that one day I would write a book on my own past lives, which I did when Penny and I moved to Georgian Bay twenty years after I read Stearn's book on the historical novelist's past lives.

Coincidences are not chance occurrences that pop into our life unbeckoned; they are divinely ordained happenstances that address our spiritual need to connect us with the story of our own journey to our true self, *the pearl of great price*. I was ready to be initiated deeper into the secret way of life; that's why I met my past-life regressionist at our first satsang of our new spiritual community in Georgian Bay.

I will talk later about how the omniscient guiding force of life opens doors for us that we did not even know existed; suffice for now to say how one of the secret doors that opened up to me when I had my past-life regressions took both me and my regressionist completely by surprise, because in my fourth regression I went back to the Body of God where I experienced myself as a soul without self-consciousness!

There, in the Body of God, I experienced myself as a single drop in the Great Ocean of Love and Mercy, but I was a new soul without a reflective sense of self; and in the same regression I was sent into the world to evolve through life as a soul seed to acquire my own identity, which I experienced in my lifetime as a higher primate with the dawning of my own reflective self-consciousness!

It was a vague and rudimentary sense of self, but as the alpha male of a group of ten or twelve higher primates I had constellated enough will power (much of which I had appropriated from my group by making them submit to my need for food and sex or suffer savage beatings) to separate from my group consciousness and realize my own distinct willful sense of self; and with the dawning of my self-consciousness I experienced the miraculous birth of a new "I" of God!

"I and my Father are one," said Jesus to the doubting Jews in the temple of Solomon in Jerusalem; but to evolve to this state of spiritual self-realization consciousness is what the journey through life is all about and the essential purpose of Christ's teaching, which he metaphorically called *the kingdom of heaven*.

It took many years to break the code of Christ's secret teaching, but with every initiation into the secret way of life I connected more dots and finally came to see that by *kingdom of heaven* Jesus meant both a *state* of spiritual self-realization consciousness and the *way* to spiritual self-realization consciousness.

In the parable of *the pearl of great price*, Jesus likens the *kingdom of heaven* unto a merchant man seeking goodly pearls; which was his way of saying that every soul in the world is in search of more life experiences (*goodly pearls*) to gain more self-consciousness until they have individuated ("acquired," as Keats put it) enough identity to want the greatest pearl of all—their true, divine self; and then like Jesus they can also say, "I and my Father are one."

And herein lies the crux of our problem, because to gain *the pearl of great price* one has to sell all that he has to purchase it; which is why Jesus said that many are called but few are chosen. Few people are willing to make this kind of sacrifice for their true self. This is what St. Paul meant in his *Letter to the Corinthians* when he said, "Ye are bought with a price," and this is the hidden message of one of Christ's most disturbing parables, the parable of the rich young ruler.

The pearl of great price costs nothing less than everything that we have, which we are not willing to pay, as the rich young man in Christ's parable proved by choosing his riches over *the kingdom of heaven*; that's why few people find their true self, and why Jesus said to his disciples that not everyone called was ready for *the kingdom of heaven*. But in the merciful Divine Plan of God, every soul will one day be made ready by the natural process of evolution through karma and reincarnation and are called again and again to seek out *the pearl of great price*, as I was in my current lifetime.

Perhaps now Shirley MacLaine's sage advice that all we really need in life is some fresh water, a good hat, and a really good pair of shoes makes infinitely good sense; because the price that we have to

pay for our true self is the karmic "baggage" of our transitory life—
all that makes us who we think we are but aren't!

3. *Feasting on the Now*

"Are you happy?" Oprah asked Shirley MacLaine in the same interview, wanting to know if she had come to terms with herself as she approached the eighth decade of her life. *"Is there a level of contentment, a sense of peace with you?"*

"O yeah," replied Shirley, with a contented smile.

But Oprah, ever-curious, probed deeper: *"In that Derek Walcott poem where he talks about sit, and feasting on your life; were you able to do that?"*

Thoughtfully, Shirley replied: *"Not so much my life. I sit and feast on the now. I really do that. And so that's why I'm so intertwined with nature; you know, my animals; my thoughts of other people. When I'm with them, I'm really feasting on the now of who they're trying to be. What an entertainment—"*

"Who they're trying to be," said the aging actress, who ironically made a guest appearance on the popular British TV drama *Downtown Abbey*, a show in which appearances take on more gravitas than reality; and she enjoyed the comedy of man's struggle with himself after years of questing for herself, which Dereck Walcott's poem that Oprah referenced speaks to—

Love after Love

The time will come
when, with elation,
you will greet yourself arriving
at your own door, in your own mirror,
and each will smile at the other's welcome
and say, sit here. Eat.
You will love again the stranger who was your self.
Give wine. Give bread. Give back your heart
to itself, to the stranger who has loved you
all your life, whom you have ignored
for another, who knows you by heart.

Take down the love letters from the bookshelf,
the photographs, the desperate notes,
peel your own image from the mirror.
Sit. Feast on your life.

"Poetry," said the American poet Adrienne Rich to Bill Moyers on PBS, "is an act of the imagination that transforms reality into a deeper perception of what is," and Derek Walcott's poem transforms the reality of man's quest for *the pearl of great price* into the deeper perception of the human condition, which is all about the unending struggle to satisfy our greatest need to be who we are meant to be.

That's how I began my quest so many years ago. I was in my early twenties when I had an experience that traumatized my conscience so badly that out of self-revulsion I sold my investment in a pool hall and vending machine business and fled to France to begin my quest for my true self, because I knew that the person who did what he did that night was not me; but I've told this story in my book *The Summoning of Noman*, so I need not expound upon it here. It's enough to know that whatever sets us on our quest for *the pearl of great price* we will all be called one day, and I was called by a totally unexpected sexual experience that brutally shocked my conscience awake from my complacent karmic slumber.

But this is how life works. When our karmic path takes us too far astray from our spiritual destiny (which is to be who we are meant to be), the firm hand of life intervenes to set us back on track; but this is so abstruse and mystifying that I cannot tell the story of my quest for my true self unless I explain what I mean by our karmic and spiritual destiny, and the omniscient guiding force of our life.

Had I not had my past-life regression to where we all come from in the Body of God and my lifetime as a higher primate where I gave birth to my reflective self, I would never have solved the mystery of our paradoxical nature; and by this I mean the paradox of our free will and pre-scripted spiritual destiny to return to God, "who is our home" as Wordsworth tells us in his poem "Intimations of Immortality"—

Our birth is but a sleep and a forgetting:
The Soul that rises with us, our life's Star,
      Hath had elsewhere its setting,
      And cometh from afar:
      Not in entire forgetfulness,
      And not in utter nakedness,
But trailing clouds of glory do we come
      From God who is our home:
Heaven lies about us in our infancy!
Shades of the prison house begin to close
      Upon the growing Boy,
But he beholds the light, and whence it flows,
      He sees it in his joy;
The Youth, who daily farther from the east
      Must travel, still is Nature's Priest,
      And by the vision splendid
      Is on his way attended;
At length the Man perceives it die away,
And fade into the light of common day.

    What William Wordsworth captured with poetic prescience, I experienced with my past-life regressions. When I was regressed to my first primordial human lifetime, I realized that the birth of my reflective self was the beginning of my karmic destiny.

    In my regression, I experienced myself in the Body of God first as a soul without reflective self-consciousness, and then I was sent into the world to evolve through life for the divinely ordained purpose of creating a new "I" of God; and from lifetime to lifetime to lifetime I grew in self-identity through the natural process of karmic evolution, which was my personally scripted destiny.

    In a letter to his brother, "The Vale of Soul Making," John Keats asked the basic question of man's existence: WHO AM I? *"There may be intelligences or sparks of divinity in millions, but they are not Souls till they acquire identities, till each one is personally itself,"* he says to his brother, sneaking a peek into the Holy Cathedral of the Divine Plan of God. *"Intelligences are atoms of perception—they know and they see and they are pure; in short, they are God. How then are Souls to be made? How then are these sparks which are God to have identity given them—so as even to possess a bliss peculiar to each one by individual existence? How but by the medium of a world like this?"*

To *be* who we are, we have to *become* who we are; that's what Keats meant by "The Vale of Soul Making." In my fourth regression, I experienced myself as "an atom of perception" in the Body of God. I knew, and I saw, and I was pure. I was an atom of God without reflective self-consciousness, a soul seed without identity, without the bliss of individual existence; and then I was sent into the world to acquire my own identity, which I did in my lifetime as a higher primate where I experienced the birth of my own reflective self that initiated my personal destiny of individuating the vital energy of life through the natural process of karma and reincarnation until I was evolved enough in my own identity to be called to seek out *the pearl of great price*, which I did in my current lifetime; and this answers the question that Jesus begs: what makes one ready for *the kingdom of heaven*?

This is the dynamic of natural evolution through karma and reincarnation, which every atom of God must experience to realize its own divine nature, and this is how I came to see that finding one's true self cannot be done in one lifetime alone. It takes many lifetimes to acquire enough self-consciousness to realize that we are more than what we think we are; only then are we called to seek out *the pearl of great price*. But to be called does not mean that we are chosen.

The rich young man in Christ's parable was ready for *the kingdom of heaven* or he would not have been called; but he chose not to pay the price for the most precious treasure in the world—his lost soul. He wasn't willing to give up his worldly riches for *the kingdom of heaven*; and so he walked away to be called another day, as is mercifully written in the Divine Plan of God.

Ironically, the rich young man did not "hear" Jesus, because it wasn't his worldly riches that Jesus asked him to give up for *the kingdom of heaven*; it was his worldly self that Buddhists call our ephemeral self. And herein lies the mystery of the secret way that Jesus gave to the world, which Shirley MacLaine intuited with her whimsical notion that *"all you really need in life is some fresh water, a good hat, and a really good pair of shoes."* After a lifetime of questing for herself, the courageous actress/seeker/writer finally met her true self and began to peel away the image of her worldly self from the mirror of her life. That's why she could feast on the now; her quest was over, and all that remained was for her to *be* herself…

4. *The Roses and the Thorns*

"Everywhere I've travelled in the world I've found that people are looking for something to fill the loneliness inside them," wrote the intrepid seeker in her memoir *I'm Over All That*; "they are after what I think of as the 'Big Truth.'"

The Big Truth is *the pearl of great price*, one's true self; and we will not rest easy until we find it. But, as Jesus said, not all of us are called to find our true self; which only adds to the mystery, because we are all teleologically driven to *become* our true self through the natural process of karma and reincarnation.

"It doesn't matter how wealthy or well suited they are," MacLaine continues; "after surface talking, joking, eating, Hollywood gossip, and cultural politeness, the conversation always turns to why are we here, what is the point of life, is God real, are we alone in the universe?" And after all was said and done, she concluded that "for us to get to the Bigger Truths, there is much for us to get over."

"Much for us to get over" is MacLaine's intuitive metaphor for letting go of that part of ourselves that inhibits our quest for *the pearl of great price*; which is why she could proudly say to Oprah that *"all you really need in life is some fresh water, a good hat, and a really good pair of shoes"*—because she had let go of all those parts of herself that kept her from *being* her true self. Which is why she found it entertaining watching people struggling with "who they're trying to be."

The struggle to be who we're trying to be is what life is all about, and some of us succeed and some of us don't (Shirley succeeded brilliantly in acting, entertaining and writing); but whether we make it or not in life does not necessarily satisfy our greatest need to be our true self. The most that life can do for us is satisfy our desire to be what we struggle to become—whether it be actor, singer, writer, surgeon, or cabinet maker—and make us ready to be called, as Carl Jung was.

Jung was the first psychologist to acknowledge the dual consciousness of our reflective self, which he identified as Personality

No 1 and Personality No. 2; but he had only conceptualized what writers have always known—writers like Goethe, whose epic tragedy *Faust* dramatizes the loss of soul; Robert Louis Stevenson, whose novel *The Strange Case of Dr. Jekyll and Mr. Hyde* magnifies the dark side of the human personality in Dr. Jekyll's Mr. Hyde; Oscar Wilde's *The Picture of Dorian Gray*, which shocked the moral sensibilities of his day; and the mystic Sufi poet Rumi, who said: "If thou hast not seen the devil, look at thine own self."

Jung called the dark side of our personality the shadow, which is the repressed, unconscious side of our ego, what he called Personality No. 1; and Personality No. 2, he called the Self, "God in us," our individuating soul Self; and integrating our two selves is at the heart of Jung's psychology of individuation. That's the secret message of Christ's teaching, which he couched in his most paradoxical saying: *"He that loveth his life shall lose it; and he that hateth his life in this world shall keep it unto life eternal."*

"The knowledge of death came to me that night," confessed Jung in *The Red Book*, as he courageously initiates himself into the secret way of life. "I went into the inner death and saw that outer dying was better than inner death. And I decided to die outside and live within…I turned away and sought the place of the inner life," thus beginning the long and slow death of his worldly self…

After living in France for a year, where I had gone to begin my quest for my true self and where I accidentally awakened the Kundalini while meditating one night which took the better part of ten years to harness, I returned to Canada and went to university to study philosophy to continue my quest; but in my second year I began to feel like I had been cast adrift in a sea of endless speculation, brilliant but philosophical speculation nonetheless, and I was so desperate that I did something that changed my life forever—I dared to pay *the* price for my true self by "dying" to my life to "find" my life.

In my second year at university I "chanced" upon Gurdjieff's teaching, which attracted me in a way that I could not fathom until I had my past-life regressions many years later when I learned that I was a student of Pythagoras and a Sufi in ancient Persia, both lifetimes that called me to seek out *the pearl of great price*, and I began to "work" on myself with Gurdjieff's teaching; but no matter how much I "worked" on myself, I couldn't quite "get" Gurdjieff's teaching, and I fell into such despair that I was compelled to take drastic measures.

I went for a long walk one weekend down the railroad tracks behind our family home to the Little Black Bridge and breakwater to the small island in the middle of the Nipigon River (Nipigon was my hometown) where I smoked half a dozen cigarettes and pondered my dilemma; and on the way back I stopped on the breakwater and looked up into the sky, and said: *"God, I know that we get nothing for nothing in this universe, or any universe for that matter; please tell me, what price truth?"* And I waited for an answer.

I didn't expect God to speak to me, but I got the answer that I pleaded for; albeit in a way that can only be described as "inspired" thought. As I waited for God's reply, I watched the fast flowing waters of the Nipigon River on their way to Lake Superior, which brought to mind the Preacher's words in The Book of Ecclesiastes: *"All the rivers run into the sea, yet the sea is not full; unto the place from whence the rivers come, thither they return again."* And then Sophocles' tragic play *Oedipus Rex* came to mind, and the thought of Oedipus's sacrifice to save his kingdom "inspired" the answer to my request, which I called my *Royal Dictum*.

My edict of self-denial came to me word perfect as I wrote it in my pocket notebook, as if dictated to me by my Higher Self: *"I am like Oedipus Rex. I am going to exile myself out of my own kingdom. I embrace my becoming blindly, and I leave all of my sins behind me. I am going to go against the natural course of evolution, and each obstacle that I encounter I will consume,"* which I vowed then and there to live for the rest of my life.

King Oedipus was true to his word. When the prophet Tiresias informed him that he was responsible for the plague that had befallen Thebes, Oedipus exiled himself according to his edict that whoever was found responsible for the plague would be banished from his kingdom.

In his arrogant youth, Oedipus unknowingly murdered his own father at a crossroads and then defiled his mother's bed by marring the murdered man's wife, and for these heinous crimes he blighted his kingdom; so he gouged out his eyes to pay for his blindness and exiled himself from his cursed kingdom, and this inspired my own exile from the kingdom of my own senses. And the moment I stepped off the breakwater onto the mainland I threw my cigarettes away and vowed to deny myself for the rest of my life all the pleasures of my life.

The logic of my *Royal Dictum* was simple, if not completely mad; but as I came to learn on my journey to my true self, the desperate seeker will pay any price for the answer they are looking for, as did the artist Jerry Wennstrom who exiled himself from the kingdom of his own life for fifteen years, as he tells us in *The Inspired Heart, An Artist's Journey of Transformation*. Like all the rivers that return to the place from whence they came, I reasoned that I would go against the currents of life by denying myself the pleasures of life in the hope of getting back to the source of my life; and my *Royal Dictum* became my edict of self-denial, thereby complying to the secret meaning of Christ's paradoxical saying that to find my life I had to die to my life.

God did "answer" me, then; and the price that I had to pay for the truth I sought was the death of my worldly life. But I would never have found *the pearl of great price* without Gurdjieff's teaching. As I began to live my life of self-denial, I soon realized that I had to be devilishly clever and immensely resourceful; and that's how I cracked the code of Gurdjieff's teaching and the paradoxical sayings of Jesus.

Gurdjieff had four basic techniques for "creating" one's own soul; *non-identifying, self-remembering, voluntary effort,* and *conscious suffering.* These techniques could be practiced anywhere anytime, and they became a way of life for me until they *became* my life; that's how I integrated the consciousness of my outer and inner self and gave birth to my immortal self, which I expressed in the following words that came to me in my self-transcendence: **I am what I am not, and I am not what I am: I am both, but neither. I am Soul.** This was my eternal self, which Jesus promised and I expounded upon in my book *Why Bother? The Riddle of the Good Samaritan* and will explain as I tell the incredible story of my quest for *the pearl of great price*...

"At first roses, roses; then thorns, thorns," said Gurdjieff, a pithy, but accurate way of describing the secret way of life according to the path he had fashioned out of all the teachings he had studied in his twenty-year quest for the meaning and purpose of life; and from the moment I connected with my inner self with my *Royal Dictum* and Gurdjieff's teaching I became elated with the joy of the roses part of my quest for my true self. But when the euphoria of finding my own way began to fade, the thorns of the self-transformation process became my life; and I suffered inordinately until I gave birth to my immortal self one summer day in my mother's kitchen while she was kneading bread dough on the kitchen table. Like a thief in the night, it stole upon me; and I *knew* that I was immortal and would never die.

The acorn seed had *become* an oak tree, and from that miraculous moment of spiritual self-realization consciousness in my mother's kitchen I no longer needed my *Royal Dictum*; and after only three and a half years I abandoned my edict of self-denial and went back into the stream of life with a joyfully buoyant sense of inner freedom.

Ironically, it was the same Book of Ecclesiastes that had inspired my *Royal Dictum* that inspired me to return to life. One night after the birth of my immortal self I was nudged to read The Book of Ecclesiastes again, and the Preacher's final words released me from my edict of self-denial that I had vowed to live for the rest of my life: *"Let us hear the conclusion of the whole matter: Fear God, and keep his commandments; for this is the whole duty of man. For God shall bring every work into judgment, with every secret thing, whether it be good, or whether it be evil."*

I put my Bible away and went out to the Nipigon Inn Hotel for my first drink of scotch whiskey in three and a half years, and another; and then I invited a young lady to come home with me, we made love, and I was back as if I had never been away…

5. *Life is Pretty Much Happenstance*

"Why are we here?" Jean Houston was asked, in one of the many interviews of her long and productive career in the human potential movement; and with an ironic twinkle, the founder of Mystery School replied: *"Maybe we're here because the selfing game is what infinity does for fun. Maybe we're here because we can ask that question, why are we here? That we've evolved to that point of self-consciousness that we're wondering where our place is in the universe. Maybe we're here because we're entering into partnership with creation itself, to evolve, to innovate, and to create new forms of creation. Ultimately, I think we're here for discovery, for evolution, for creating emergent new forms in this universe of infinite forms, and to be conscious of the task."*

Jean Houston *knows*. Her own path, however she defines it, has initiated her into the secret way, and she no longer speculates about the meaning and purpose of life because she is a *knower* of the mystery; and like all initiates of the secret way, she gives intuitive expression to the mystery in the mythic language of her own *enlightened* path, and she does so with the gift of entertainment that she inherited from her talented father who wrote for comedians like Bob Hope and the ventriloquist Edgar Bergen (the actress Candice Bergen's father) and his wisecracking little wooden dummy Charlie McCarthy.

All initiates of the secret way fascinate me, but Jean Houston charmed me with her gift of avuncular storytelling; especially her story of one of the most remarkable happenstances in the history of happenstances, which speaks to what I inevitably had to call the omniscient guiding force of life that calls us to our destiny. Jean was called at the tender age of eight when her father said to her one day, *"Hey kid, you want to come and talk to Charlie?"*

Jean loved talking to Charlie McCarthy, and she jumped at the opportunity; which, as she tells Jeffrey Mishlove on his show *Thinking Allowed*, turned out to be *"one of the most thrilling things that happened to me,"* little realizing that the happenstance that she was about to experience would be her life's calling.

"*Let's go, Daddy,"* she said, all excited; and her father took her to Edgar Bergen's hotel room. The door was open, so they walked in because they heard voices; and there was Bergen and little Charlie McCarthy with their back to them talking. Jean and her father listened quietly to a conversation that shocked Jean's father but touched his young daughter's soul so deeply that it set the course of her life.

Bergen was asking his wooden dummy ultimate questions, like: *"Charlie, what is the nature of life? Charlie, what does it mean to be truly good? Charlie, where is the soul?"* And Jean Houston, animated by the memory of her childhood experience, relates the whole story to Mishlove: *"This little dummy was answering with the wisdom of the universe. It was as if all the greatest philosophical minds of five millennium were condensed inside that little wooden head and coming out of those little wooden jaws; and Bergen got so excited at these extraordinary numinous answers that he said, 'But Charlie, how can we really know anything? Charlie, what or who is God?' And the little dummy would listen and pour out these incredible gems of high-crafted wisdom; and my father, who was an agnostic Baptist, got very embarrassed by these answers, and he coughed; and Bergen turned around and turned beet red, and said, 'Hello Jack, hi Jean; I see you caught us.' And my father said, 'Ed, what are you doing? I didn't write that stuff. You're rehearsing, aren't you?' And Bergen replied, 'No rehearsal, Jack. This is real. I was asking Charlie the most important questions, and you heard the answers; and my father said, 'But that's you. That's your voice. That's your knowledge coming out of that dummy's mouth. And Bergen said, 'Well, yes; I suppose ultimately it is; but you know, when I ask him these questions and he answers, I haven't got the faintest idea what he's going to say. And what he says astounds me with his wisdom. It is so much more than I know.'* <u>*And I could feel, I as a little child of eight years old, felt as if my whole future was condensed in that moment*</u>, *that as we are, compared to the way we think we are, we inhabit such a tiny part of our reality, maybe the attic of ourselves,* *with the first, second, and third and fourth floor relatively uninhabited, and the basement locked, except occasionally when it explodes; <u>and from that moment my life, in a sense my life course was set; because I knew that I had to devote my life to helping people access these extraordinary domains of knowledge, of potential that we all have but have shut ourselves off from</u>…"*

I couldn't suppress my laughter at the irony of a wooden dummy answering the ultimate questions of life with the wisdom of the universe; but to an eight-year old Jean Houston Charlie McCarthy was much more than a wooden dummy. He was the wise Wizard of Oz speaking to her soul, and she heard the call to her destiny which many years later she amplified in her wonderful book *The Wizard of Us*.

But as fascinating as the happenstance of Jean Houston's experience with the preternaturally gifted Edgar Bergen and his wooden dummy was, it was no less fascinating than the happenstance that sparked the fire in fifteen-year old Frank Langella's soul when he just happened to see Marilyn Monroe one day in New York City.

In his juicy memoir *Dropped Names*, the laudable stage and screen actor tells the story of how he felt trapped in Bayonne, New Jersey; and that his chance encounter with Marilyn Monroe in New York City felt like lightening had struck when she said "Hi" to "a small, skinny kid in horned-rimmed glasses born into a middle-class Italian family feeling always like I didn't belong."

Marilyn Monroe's simple "Hi" was Frank Langella's call to become an actor. "What were the odds of this chance encounter?" he writes. "She was my first Someone existing outside my prison walls. An ineffable creature, stopping for an instant, looking directly into the eyes of a fifteen-year old boy, smiling, and speaking just one word. One was enough. Lightning had struck."

But why did young Frank venture out into New York City that day? What nudged him to explore the city? He tells us: "An indefinable yearning to free myself from a life I instinctively felt was killing my soul had caused me to venture forth that day without guidance or direction; not so much from bravery as from desperation."

Though not as dramatic as my sexual experience that compelled me to venture out into the world to free myself from myself, young Frank Langella was called to his true self no less than I was, as was eight-year old Jean Houston and every person that is ready to find their own path to their true self; because this is how the natural law of spiritual growth works to bring one's karmic destiny into agreement with their spiritual destiny, and fight it as most of us do, it will drag us all the same as the Stoic philosopher Cleanthes tells us in *Hymn to Zeus*:

> Lead me, Zeus, and you too, Destiny,
> To wherever your decrees have assigned me.
> I follow readily, but if I choose not,
> Wretched though I am, I must follow still.
> Fate guides the willing, but drags the unwilling.

"Life is pretty much happenstance," said Frank Langella on the *Charlie Rose* show as he talked about his memoir *Dropped Names*; and the older one gets the more one sees this to be true.

There are any number of books that attest to this inscrutable fact of life— *There Are No Accidents: Synchronicity and the Stories of Our Lives*, by Robert H. Hopcke; *The Power of Coincidence: How Life Shows Us What We Need to Know,* by David Richo; and *Soul Moments: Marvelous Stories of Synchronicity*, by Phil Cousineau, to name only a few; but I can't help but relate one more story of miraculous happenstance that I heard on the radio first and then read in the legendary jazz musician Herbie Hancock's autobiography, *Possibilities*. Of all the happenstances that I've read about, this one spoke the language of life so beautifully that it literally gave me goose bumps.

Herbie Hancock was in his early twenties, onstage at a concert hall in Stockholm, Sweden, in the mid-1960s playing piano with the Miles Davies Quintet that he had been with for a couple of years: "The band is tight—we're all in sync, all on the same wavelength.

The music is flowing, we're connecting with the audience, and everything feels magical, like we're weaving a spell."

They were playing one of Miles's classics, "So What?" The audience was on the edge of their seats: "Miles starts playing, building up to his solo, and just as he's about to really let loose, he takes a breath. And right then I play a chord that is just *so* wrong. I don't even know where it came from—it's the wrong chord, in the wrong place, and now it's hanging out there like a piece of rotten fruit."

Herbie's wrong chord just happened. He didn't know where it came from; but what turned it into the miraculous happenstance that called Herbie to the path that defined his musical destiny was how the virtuoso and initiate of the secret way Miles Davies took that wrong chord and made it right.

"It took me years to fully understand what happened in that moment on stage," Herbie wrote in his autobiography. "As soon as I played that chord I judged it. In my mind it was the 'wrong' chord. But Miles never judged it—he just heard it as a sound that had happened, and he instantly took it on as a challenge, a question of *How can I integrate that chord into everything else we're doing?* And because he didn't judge it, he was able to run with it, to turn it into something amazing"—just as I *had* to do with my "wrong" sexual experience.

That wrong chord was Herbie Hancock's initiation into the secret way through his chosen profession, because every path can be an entry point into the secret way of life,; but only because he had a mentor that took that wrong chord and opened up a gateway to the secret way for the young musician to enter.

In the dressing room after the show, Herbie asked Miles about it; but Miles just smiled and winked. "He didn't say anything. He didn't have to," wrote Herbie; and he took the lesson to heart and initiated himself into the secret way, and in time he too would show a young musician the gateway to the secret way just as Miles had shown him and as that strange and mysterious teacher Michael who appeared out of nowhere taught the young Victor L. Wooten everything that he had to know about music to initiate himself into the secret way which he wrote about in his incredible story *The Music Lesson, A Spiritual Search for Growth Through Music.*

As he reflected on his long and successful career, Herbie Hancock reveals what every initiate of the secret way comes to realize—that the path to one's true self is without exception the road less traveled by, as Robert Frost immortalized in his iconic poem *The Road Not Taken*: "Two roads diverged in a wood, and I— /I took the one less travelled by, /And that has made all the difference."

"We all have a natural human tendency to take the safe route—to do the things we know will work—rather than taking a chance," Herbie sums up in the story of his life. "But that's the antithesis of jazz, which is all about being in the present. Jazz is about being in the moment, at every moment. It's about trusting yourself to respond on the fly (as his mentor Miles did). If you allow yourself to do that, you never stop exploring, you never stop learning, in music or in life."

That's the secret way of life…

6. *The Tragedy of Effort*

"I have pissed out more life than you have lived," said my literary mentor and high school hero Ernest Hemingway in a dream one night while I was living in Annecy, France in my early twenties; and from his tortured and conflicted life I learned *the* most important lesson about the paradoxical nature of man which I explored in my book *The Lion that Swallowed Hemingway*: I learned about *the tragedy of effort.*

After I dropped out of university in my third year of philosophy studies, I began to forge my own path in life with Gurdjieff's teaching of "work on oneself," and the more I "worked" on myself the more I began to sense the secret way of life.

In his commentary to Richard Wilhelm's translation of *The Secret of the Golden Flower*, Carl Jung wrote: "when I began my lifework in the practice of psychiatry and psychotherapy, I was completely ignorant of Chinese philosophy, and only later did my professional experience show me that in my technique I had been unconsciously led along the secret way which has been the preoccupation of the best minds of the East for centuries."

Carl Jung began to sense the secret way in his practice, just as I began to sense the secret way of life in my house-painting business that I started when I left university; and the more I "worked" on myself with my *Royal Dictum* and Gurdjieffian techniques of *non-identifying, self-remembering, voluntary effort*, and *conscious suffering* the more the secret way revealed itself to me. But this requires explanation, because few people can articulate the secret way of life that is everywhere to be found; not even gifted writers like Ernest Hemingway whose literary credo to "tell it as it was" connected him with the life force (which he called "juice") and awakened him to the secret way.

Mary Hemingway, Ernest's fourth and last wife, quotes her husband in her memoir *How It Was*: "Nobody really knows or understands and nobody has ever said the secret. The secret is that it is poetry written into prose, and it is the hardest of all things to do."

Jung too, just before he died, confessed to Miguel Serrano (*C. G. Jung and Hermann Hesse, A Record of Two Friendships*) that only a poet could understand the mystery of the secret way; but even the poets in all their genius have failed to explain the mystery of the secret way of life.

Like Jung and Hemingway, many people can sense the secret way in their work; but their understanding of the secret way depends entirely upon their level of initiation in life; so some give us glimpses of the secret way, and others open the doors of the soul so wide that we drown in the wisdom that pours out of them—like Rumi did with his poetry. Of all the poets, Rumi is the most discursive on the secret way of life; but, still, he does not really tell us what it is.

Because I "worked" on myself with such pathological commitment, I was pulled so deep into the mystery of the secret way that I began to "see" the secret way everywhere, especially in the sayings and parables of Jesus; and as I *lived* the secret way according to Jesus, which I incorporated into my personal path, I awakened to the mystery of the secret way of life and finally understood what Gurdjieff meant by calling his teaching "esoteric Christianity." But, again, this is so difficult to explain that I have to beg the reader's indulgence...

According to Gurdjieff, Nature can only evolve us so far and no further; and to evolve to our highest potential we have to take evolution into our own hands. This was the purpose of both Gurdjieff's system and Christ's teaching—to give us the means to realize our highest potential, which Jesus called *the pearl of great price.*

However he came to his belief that not everyone is born with an immortal soul, Gurdjieff believed that we can create our own soul with relentless conscious effort, which was the premise of his system; but whether one believed Gurdjieff or not, his system worked all the same, to which I can attest with the birth of my own immortal self in my mother's kitchen that fine summer day so many years ago.

My spiritual rebirth was in reality the *becoming* of one self out of my two selves, just as Jesus promised when he was asked by someone when his kingdom would come: *"When the two will be one, and the outer like the inner, and the male with the female neither male nor female."* And Thomas goes on to say in the *Gospel of Thomas*, "Now the two are one when we speak truth to each other and there is one soul in two bodies with no hypocrisy."

"One soul in two bodies with no hypocrisy." This is the mystery of Christ's teaching of spiritual rebirth, and Gurdjieff's system despite his premise that we are not all born with an immortal soul, and which also became central to Jung's psychology of individuation that speaks to the secret way of life.

The two bodies are Jung's Personality No. 1, and Personality No. 2. These two bodies are the outer and inner self, and by one soul is meant the transformation of the outer and inner self into one transcendent Self; but this self-transformation is so difficult to realize that Jesus referred to it as *the pearl of great price.*

The pearl of great price is the individuated consciousness of our divine self; but to realize our divine self we have to *become* our divine self with relentless conscious effort, which is what makes it so difficult to realize. "Man must finish the work which Nature has left incomplete," said the Alchemists; which means that we have to live our life in such a way as to blend (the "sacred marriage" of Alchemy) the consciousness of our outer self with the consciousness of our inner self and create a consciousness of one harmonious self. This is the premise of my literary memoir *The Lion that Swallowed Hemingway*.

The Lion that Swallowed Hemingway is the story of my own individuation process, but Hemingway and Jung are my two principal characters that illustrate the failure and success of the process of individuation. Hemingway's life illustrates *the tragedy of effort*; and Jung's life illustrates *the triumph of effort*—because Hemingway died a tragic suicide brought on by the conflict of his two selves, and Jung died triumphant in the realization of his wholeness and singleness of self.

In *Our Dreaming Mind*, Robert L. Van de Castle wrote: "By following the messages appearing in dreams, Jung believed that the path leading to self-realization and personal wholeness could be realized. His belief was affirmed in a dream he experienced just before his death. In it he saw, 'high up in a high place,' a boulder lit by the full sun. Carved into the illuminated boulder were the words 'Take this as a sign of the wholeness you have achieved and the singleness you have become.'"

Jung and Hemingway speak to the paradoxical nature of man, Hemingway living his life in the tortured conflict of his paradoxical self, and Jung living his life in the valiant effort to resolve the conflict of his paradoxical self; and by paradoxical self I mean the *being* and *non-being* of our individuating self-consciousness.

And this is where I part company with the world in my understanding of the individuation process, because in my quest for my true self I came to see that there are two ways that lead to *the pearl of great price*—the way of *non-being*, which is the way of the world; and the way of *being,* which is the way of Divine Spirit.

But the way of *non-being* cannot complete the process of individuation, and leads inevitably to *the tragedy of effort* because the way of the world is the way of karma and reincarnation which cannot transcend our two selves. The most that the way of the world can do is make one ready to be called to their destiny, as I was called in my current lifetime when I vowed to find my true self or die trying.

No matter how successful the way of the world may be—Carl Jung achieved everything that he dreamt of by the age of forty, and Ernest Hemingway was driven to be the best writer of his generation and was awarded the Nobel Prize for Literature in 1954—the way of the world cannot realize the full potential of our life that Jesus called *the pearl of great price*, which is the individuated consciousness of our *being* and *non-being* and our true self. But why?

Because the way of the world cannot complete what Nature cannot finish. The way of world is the way of karma and reincarnation, and unless one makes a conscious effort to resolve the selfish attitude of his worldly self that keeps him from transcending himself, he will never realize his full potential and find *the pearl of great price*. This is why Jesus said, *"He that loveth his life shall lose it, and he that hateth his life in this world shall keep it unto life eternal."*

Hemingway took the way of the world and lusted for life. He loved to eat, drink, hunt, fish, and have sex both in and out of marriage; and he wrote about the way of the world with such artistic integrity that he inspired generations of writers, and he was rewarded with the most prestigious prize in literature for his effort; but the way of the world also drove him to chronic depression, paranoia, and suicide.

Hemingway had a monstrous dark side to his ego personality. So powerful was his shadow side that when it took over his personality he became insufferable to be with, especially when he was drinking. His third wife Martha Gellhorn called him a pathological liar and the cruelest man she knew, but only because he did not have it in him to resolve the dark side of his unconscionably selfish personality.

His whole life Hemingway wanted to have his cake and eat it too, which is a phenomenal trick that can only be accomplished when one lives by the values of the secret way as Jung did and wrote about with uncanny insight on the enantiodromiac nature of man, because the secret way transforms the false consciousness of our *non-being* and makes our two selves into one—"one soul in two bodies with no hypocrisy." So what is the secret way? What is this mysterious dynamic that transforms our life and brings us closer to our true self?

Hemingway caught a glimpse of the secret in his writing, which he allegorized in Santiago's struggle in *The Old Man and the Sea*, and Jung discovered it in his practice; but what is this elusive dynamic that plays hide and seek with us? What is its magic, which has the power to satisfy the longing for our true self more than any passion for life, which was why my literary mentor said that he loved writing more than any other pleasure he got from life, including sex and deep sea fishing?

If I hadn't experienced the satisfaction that writing gave me, I would never have understood how Hemingway could say that he loved writing even more than sex or fishing for marlin off his beloved boat *Pilar* in the Gulf Coast, which he did with lustful abandon; but because I lived the secret way consciously, I knew where Hemingway was coming from, and I no longer harbor resentment for his cocky remark in my dream in Annecy, France. He might have pissed out more life than I had lived, but I didn't come back into this world to live all the life I could (I had lived that kind of self-indulgent life in Paris in the 17th Century); I came into the world to find my true self. That's why I became a seeker at such an early age in my current life.

But it took a long time for me to understand that the way of the world is necessary for our journey to *the pearl of great price*, because only by getting the most out of life can we grow in the consciousness of our own identity, which casts a whole new light on the ego that has always been misunderstood by the world, especially religion.

Ego is the driving force of Personality No. 1, and the more ego-driven we are, the more vital life force we get from life, which we need to grow in self-identity. And when we have grown enough in our own identity to realize that we are more than our ego personality, we are called to our own path by the divine law of synchronicity.

And the more true we are to our own path, be it writing, art, music, medicine, or whatever, the more we grow in who we are meant to be until life can no longer satisfy our longing for our true self through our ego personality and we are called by the divine law of synchronicity to become seekers. And then one day we will be initiated into the secret way and tap directly into the inherently self-transcending energy of the *Creative Life Stream* that flows back home to God; and that's how we find *the pearl of great price…*

7. *Drawing the Line*

John Updike, one of America's distinguished men of letters who mastered the short story, novel, poetry, and personal essay drew the line early in his long and celebrated career: *"My duty as a writer is to make the best record I can of life as I understand it, and that duty takes precedence for me over all other considerations."*

But then late in life, tired from the oppressive responsibility of the creative process, "hovering always near a greatness he is too shrewd or diffident to risk," according to Professor Harold Bloom, Updike said about writing: "We walk through volumes of the unexpressed and like snails leave behind a faint thread excreted out of ourselves," which was his humorous, albeit cynical way of saying that all writing, including his own, was crap; and it may very well be in the grand scheme of things, but if it weren't for the stories that writers write, how would we learn about the human condition—like Updike's *Rabbit* series of novels that opened up a window onto the life of ordinary man?

A writer's job is to tell the truth, as every writer knows; but telling the truth comes with a heavy price, because the truth can be too much for most people to bear. This is where Updike excelled, because he had the talent to couch his truth well but yet shine a telling light onto the prosaic life of Middle America as he did in his many *New Yorker* stories, and especially in his scandalous novel *Couples* that made his remarkable career. And yet, when a writer cuts too close to the bone it can shock the reader's psyche; as happened to me…

Over the years I've come to believe that a writer does not choose the books he writes; rather, they choose him. This happenstance began with my first book, a novel memoir arrogantly titled *What Would I Say Today If I Were to Die Tomorrow?*

Laying on the couch perusing my QPB book club selections, I came across Ruth Picardie's *Before I Say Goodbye*, the true story of the final year of her cancer-stricken life; and in one sudden burst of inspiration the title of my own before-I-say-goodbye book came to me, and I wrote: "The first thing I would say today if I were to die tomorrow would be this: *We live more than one life, and it is foolish to deny this simple truth."* Talk about drawing a line!

Obviously, reincarnation was no longer a belief for me; it had become my truth, and I dared to tell the world that it was foolish to deny the fact that when we die we return to live life over again to grow and evolve accordingly; and if that wasn't enough, the second thing I dared to tell the world was: *"Self-deception is our greatest threat to personal growth, happiness, and wholeness."*

Nothing has happened to change my mind since I wrote that book thirteen years ago; if anything, life has confirmed my truth almost to the point of despair, because the more I see of life the more convinced I am that stupidity is not a gift of God but entirely man-made. But my novel stunned my hometown, and Penny and I had to relocate to Georgian Bay for peace of mind.

Like Thomas Wolfe, who shocked his hometown of Ashville, North Carolina with his first novel *Look Homeward, Angel* and went back eight years later to get material for his novel *You Can't Go Home Again,* I also went back to my hometown eleven years later to resolve some personal issues and get material for my novel-in-progress, *We May be Tiny, But We're Not Small,* an ironic play on words because we live in the county of Tiny Township in Georgian Bay. So by drawing the line I was forced to step out of the suffocating little box of my old life in my hometown of Nipigon, Northwestern Ontario and into the paradigm of my new life in Georgian Bay; and that, as Robert Frost would say, "has made all the difference."

By the time I wrote my first novel, I had "worked" on myself for many years; and I had acquired what can only be called a sixth sense. I could "see" a person's shadow; and, as strange as this may sound, a person's shadow would sense that I could see it. This was cause for tension in my relationships, because the shadow does not like to be seen. Its power lies in not being seen, and it felt threatened.

It takes great moral courage to see the shadow, said Carl Jung; and I had incorporated the Socratic ethos of living by the noble virtues to "gather and collect" my soul back into itself from the depths of my unconscious shadow; so I understood why a person's shadow would be threatened by me, and I had to adjust my attitude with people accordingly: the darker the shadow, the more careful I had to be.

Carl Jung, who by the age of sixty had "swallowed" his own shadow, had the same threatening effect on people. "The unconscious of people who live in an artificial manner sense in me a danger. Everything about me irritates them, my way of speaking, my way of laughing," I read in Claire Dunne's elegant and concise biography *Wounded Healer of the Soul* when we moved to Georgian Bay, confirming what I could not reveal at the time, let alone explain—

"What the fuck are you trying to prove out there, anyway?" said an old Finnish resident of my hometown in the post office one freezing January morning, referring to my long distance runs along the Lake Helen shoreline in weather so cold that icicles hung off the face mask I had fashioned out of my drywall dust mask to put over the mouth of my balaclava to protect my lungs from the freezing air.

"Nothing. I love to run," I replied, knowing how futile it would be to explain to him that I had incorporated long distance running into my Gurdjieffian program of "work" on myself, and which proved to be so effective that I grew in my true self exponentially in my *voluntary effort* and *conscious suffering* by running in such foul weather.

"Are you crazy, running in this weather? What are you, some kind of nut?" said the disgruntled old-timer.

"To each his own," I said, and walked away.

Which made my private life as a housepainter in Nipigon very interesting, because I had to "work" in people's homes; and I painted a lot of houses in my hometown. So by the time I wrote *What Would I Say Today If I Were to Die Tomorrow?* I was very familiar with the shadow personality of my hometown, and when people recognized the real life models for my fictional characters in my novel the whole town rallied against me in their collective shadow mentality; just as they did to Thomas Wolfe when he wrote *Look Homeward, Angel*.

Curiously enough, the same thing happened to my literary hero whose first novel turned Hemingway's friends that had inspired the "lost generation" in *The Sun Also Rises* against the brazen author; and one man (Harold Loeb who became Robert Cohn) was wounded so badly by how he was portrayed, especially his fawning behavior with Lady Brett Ashely, that he was still smarting fifty years later. And this speaks to the power of the false side of our personality that will do anything to keep from being exposed to the light of day, which any writer worth their salt has to do to tell their truth about life—

"What do the people of your hometown think of your writing?" Shelagh Rogers, host of CBC's *The Next Chapter*, asked Alice Munroe two or three years before she was awarded the Nobel Prize for Literature in 2013.

"I don't know. They don't speak to me," replied Munroe, who wrote many stories inspired by people from her hometown and the Huron County; which helped to ameliorate the pain that Penny and I had to suffer from the people of my hometown and surrounding area.

Our shadow is a mysterious creature; it neither is nor is not. It is the unresolved self of our ego personality, and inauthentic; but it is real all the same, as Robert Louis Stevenson captured in his groundbreaking novel *The Strange Case of Dr. Jekyll and Mr. Hyde*. And not until we have resolved the *non-being* of our shadow self will we be who we are meant to be; which Gurdjieff's teaching taught me how to do.

But Gurdjieff's teaching wasn't enough. As effective as his techniques of *non-identifying, self-remembering, voluntary effort,* and *conscious suffering* were, they lacked the power of self-transcendence. They only had the power to harness the vital life force and transform the consciousness of my shadow self, which was not enough to satisfy my teleological imperative to *become* my true self.

That's why I got pulled into the secret way of Christ's teaching, and the secret way of everyday life wherever I discerned it, as I did in Wordsworth's poem "Character of the Happy Warrior" whose iconic two lines became my ideal: "He labors good on good to fix, and owes /To virtue every triumph that he knows."

I had to draw the line every hour of every day to satisfy the longing in my soul for my true self, but I had to pay a price to "gather and collect" myself into myself, as Socrates expressed what Jung called the *"transcendent function"* of the secret way.

In Plato's *Phaedo*, Socrates reveals the secret way: "And what is purification but the separation of the soul from the body, as I was saying before; the habit of soul gathering and collecting herself into herself, out of all the courses of the body; the dwelling in her own place alone, as in another life, so also in this, as far as she can; the release of the soul from the chains of the body?"

That's the mysterious dynamic of the secret way, to release the soul from the chains of the body and transcend ourselves; and one day we will all have to draw the line and live the path that we have been called to, because that's the only way we can engage the *transcendent function* and tap into the *Creative Life Stream* that will release us from the chains of our body and complete what Nature cannot finish.

As St. Paul said in his *Letter to the Philippians*, "Wherefore, my beloved, as ye have always obeyed, not as in my presence only, but now much more in my absence, work out your own salvation with fear and trembling," so too must we "work" on ourselves to *become* who we are meant to be. This is the secret of the secret way…

8. *When Life Is Not Enough*

How I wanted a personal mentor in my life, a flesh and bones person who could guide me through life's uneasy ways; but my calling was to forge my own path, which I did with such naiveté that it sends shivers up my spine today whenever I think about it. But I had a raw, visceral courage and faith in myself that offset my dangerous innocence, and I have no doubt that God guided every step of my way to my true self.

The quest for one's true self is a long and lonely journey. Out of the thousands of birds that went on the quest for God in the Sufi poet Farid ud-Din Attar's allegory *The Conference of the Birds*, only thirty succeed to look into the Face of God; and to their astonishment, they saw their own image. I was one of the thirty birds; but ten years after the most ineffable experience of my life, doubt assailed me.

But again, God saved me from myself when the merciful law of divine synchronicity called me to an experience one Sunday morning on my run down Highway 11 along the shoreline of Lake Helen in my hometown of Nipigon when I came upon a flock of Canada geese resting on the sandy shore along the full length of an ashen grey weather-beaten driftwood tree—

"God, wouldn't it be something if there were thirty birds there?" I exclaimed to myself, vainly hoping to give symbolic confirmation to my experience of having looked into the Face of God; and I stopped to count the birds.

I counted twenty-five, and my heart sank; but then I counted again, just to make sure, and I counted twenty-seven. I climbed upon the guardrail for a better look, and I spotted two more crouched in the roots of the tree, which made twenty-nine and one short of my symbolic confirmation. I counted three more times, but there were only twenty-nine birds and I felt like God had abandoned me; so I jumped off the guard rail and resumed my run to Five Mile Park, but no sooner did I take five or six strides and it hit me— "I'M THE THIRTIETH BIRD!"

I never again doubted my experience, which confirmed what I should have known long ago when I took to heart Blavatsky's words in *The Voice of the Silence*: "The Mind is the great Slayer of the Real. Let the Disciple slay the Slayer," and I trusted myself all the more after the synchronistic confirmation of my experience of looking into the Face of God; which was why I gravitated to John Updike's novel *Seek My Face* at a book fair in the Bayfield Mall in Barrie, Ontario when I was working on *Healing with Padre Pio*, because *Seek My Face* coincidentally pointed to my conviction that **all art seeks the Face of God**.

Updike quotes Psalm 27 as an epigram for his novel— *"You speak in my heart and say, "Seek my face." Your face, Lord, will I seek"*—thereby setting the tone of his creative inquiry into the life of seventy-eight year old painter Hope Chafetz, who was modeled on the famous abstract artist Jackson Pollock's wife to satisfy Updike's haunting curiosity about the creative process, because like Hemingway he too had caught a glimpse of that mystical secret that Hemingway hinted at when he said that nobody really knows or understands the secret and that it was poetry written into prose and the hardest of all things to do, which only challenged the enormously talented Updike who called the secret "it" in *Rabbit, Run* and whose literary ethos was to "lift the ordinary into the eternal realm of art," and "give the mundane its beautiful due" because he could see that "it" was the magic ingredient of life.

Seek My Face was Updike's literary effort to come to terms with the creative process, the beauty of being, and the individual self; but, sadly, neither the gifted poet, the novelist, nor the artist have been able to resolve the secret "it" that drives them all to seek the Face of God; but that's only because they cannot engage their *transcendent function* enough to integrate their inner and outer self and awaken to their divine nature, because if they could they would become one of the thirty birds in the poet's allegory and bask in the bliss of their wholeness and singleness of self.

But why can't they? This question haunts all artists; but it was intuitively answered by the gifted New Zealand writer Katherine Mansfield when she shared her views on the creative process with her mentor A. R. Orage when she was living at Gurdjieff's Institute for the Harmonious Development of Man in Fontainebleau, France shortly before she died of tuberculosis at the age of thirty-four.

"Literature is not enough," said Katherine to A.R. Orage, the brilliant editor of Britain's *New Age* journal who quit his exciting literary life to follow the enigmatic Gurdjieff for the rest of his life. "Suppose that I could succeed in writing as well as Shakespeare. It would be lovely, but what then? There is something wanting in literary art, even at its highest. **Literature is not enough**," confessed Mansfield, which was what attracted her to Gurdjieff's teaching.

Mansfield's writing had taken her as far as her creative path could take her, but it wasn't enough to satisfy the longing in her soul. "One must become more to write better," she concluded, and she felt that Gurdjieff could teach her how to become more; but sadly she died before she could satisfy her hunger to become the person she longed to be. But as Orage tells us in his little book *On Love,* Katherine Mansfield managed to catch a glimpse of the secret way by "working" on herself with Gurdjieff's teaching: **she had to change her attitude about life.**

"Could we change our attitude, we should not only see life differently, but life itself could *be* different. Life would undergo a change of appearance because we ourselves had undergone a change in attitude," she tells Orage; which was why she was pulled into Gurdjieff's teaching in search of a higher path.

But Katherine Mansfield wasn't the only artist whose path could not satisfy the longing in their soul to be all they were driven to be by the imperative of their own path; Jerry Wennstorm suffered the same creative fate when his art brought him as far as it could take him, and he gave up painting to heed the call of Soul and take up the dangerous path of "letting go and letting God."

"I trusted a higher good that I sensed was much better equipped to inform my choices than anything I had available in the limited range of will and intelligence," he wrote in *The Inspired Heart, An Artist's Journey of Transformation,* because he had come to the tragic realization that **art was not enough** to satisfy the longing in his soul to be all that he could be; and for fifteen years he lived on the serendipitous bounty of providential guidance. Again, talk about drawing the line!

    But that's the price that one is willing to pay when they are called to a higher path, as my hero Carl Gustav Jung did when he was called to the higher path of integrating his Personality No. 1 with his Personality No. 2; just as I was called to my higher path when I was inspired to create my *Royal Dictum.*

    In his lovely biography simply called *Updike*, Adam Begley tells us that in a draft ending that was eventually dropped from his memoir *Self-Consciousness*, John Updike "conceded that he was peddling a kind of 'cagey candor' and proposed that the title of the book should be *Self-Serving*, or *Self-Promotion*," illustrating with artistic integrity just how difficult it is to be totally truthful with oneself and why I wrote that self-deception is our greatest threat to personal growth, happiness, and wholeness.

    Even so, being totally truthful with oneself (as far as this is possible, because it takes great courage to strip away the many layers of one's own vanity) we can never satisfy the longing in our soul to be all that we are meant to be until we take evolution into our own hands and complete what Nature cannot finish; and whenever I watch an old Updike interview on the Internet, I am touched by the aura of tragedy that he projected. Despite the full and satisfying life that he lived, the great author's life was sadly incomplete; and the magnificent failure of his attempt to resolve the deepest issue of his own identity through his poetry, short stories, novels, and essays moves me to tears…

9. "Creation's Giddy Bliss"

Why does a writer *have* to write? John Updike *had* to write. It sustained him body and soul. Why does an artist *have* to paint? Jerry Wennstrom *had* to paint until it no longer sustained him and he had to seek a higher path. Why does a musician *have* to play music? Herbie Hancock *has* to play. Jazz nourishes his soul. Why does the artist *have* to do what they are called to do by their art, be it writing, painting, music or whatever? That's the secret power of "it" that digs its tentacles into one's soul and won't let them go unto they satisfy their longing to be more.

In the late fall of 2005, four years before his death, John Updike complained to his friend and fellow writer Joyce Carol Oates, "I find producing anything fraught with difficulty these days, and tinged with a certain word-disgust, for which there must be an excellent German term." As tired as he was of writing, even in his despair Updike never tired of "creation's giddy bliss" that writing gave him; that's the secret power of "it" that nourishes the artist's soul and drives them to create.

I'm a writer, and I know about "creation's giddy bliss." But I was a seeker also, and in my quest to resolve the deepest issue of my identity which was foisted upon me when my shadow came out one night after I closed down my pool hall business for the day and compelled me to have a sexual experience that brutally shocked my conscience awake, I learned that this magical "it" was everywhere to be found; and all one had to do to tap into the power of "creation's giddy bliss" was to engage their *transcendent function.*

Katherine Mansfield figured it out. She realized that it was her own attitude that kept her from becoming the person she longed to be; that's why she began to "work" on herself with Gurdjieff's remarkable teaching at his Institute in Fontainebleau, France.

The *transcendent function* is a term created by Carl Jung for the individuation process of integrating our inner and outer self; but the *transcendent function* of Mansfield's writing could no longer satisfy the longing in her soul to be all that she could be, and she had to seek a higher path as every person must when their *transcendent function* ceases to satisfy the longing in their soul.

But it takes enormous courage to seek a higher path when one's own path can no longer satisfy their longing to be more, which is why so many writers get beaten up by life; like Hemingway, whose monstrous shadow swallowed him whole and destroyed his adventuresome manly life. That's the secret of the *transcendent function* that I expound upon in *The Lion that Swallowed Hemingway*; the secret power of "it" that I discovered as I "worked" on myself with Gurdjieff's system, my *Royal Dictum*, and the cryptic sayings of Jesus…

David Foster Wallace, an unusually gifted young writer who meanly snapped at the ankles of "the Great Male Narcissists" (Mailer, Roth, and Updike) but who failed to engage his *transcendent function* enough to keep his suicidal shadow in check, wrote an animus-laced review for *The New York Observer* of Updike's novel *Toward the End of Time*; but he too had experienced the secret power of "it" whenever he wrote, because the *transcendent function* of his writing kept him from spiraling into depression that finally swallowed him whole and compelled him to take his own life by hanging. A sad, but not surprising ending to a very gifted writer.

But that's not uncommon in the world of art when the artist fails to resolve the conflicted nature of their inner and outer self. On the *Charlie Rose* show David Foster Wallace revealed the great distance that he had to travel to get to his true self, and he foreshadowed his tragic demise when he told Charlie Rose that he feared explaining his rationale for the extensive endnotes for his mammoth 1100 page novel *Infinite Jest* because he didn't want to look pretentious talking about it, and Charlie Rose, with an amused smile, interrupted Wallace and said, "Quit worrying about how you're going to look and just *be*." But this innocent simple wisdom only triggered more anxiety.

The distance between *appearance* and *being* is what the journey to one's true self is all about, and David Foster Wallace, who had a history of depression and mental breakdowns and shock therapy, could not to be true to the *transcendent function* of his creative imperative and bridge the chasm that separated his two selves; and like my literary mentor Wallace fell into such despair that he could not pull himself out of the dark recesses of his self-destructive inauthentic shadow life.

As I watched David Foster Wallace on *Charlie Rose*, wearing a bandanna on his head because acutely self-conscious anxiety caused him to sweat profusely, I realized something that I simply did not want to acknowledge: regardless how talented and brilliant a writer may be, and everyone hailed DFW to be a literary genius, literature would never be enough to bridge the chasm that divides our two selves, because it takes more than the creative process to engage the *transcendent function* enough to resolve our two selves and the central issue of the human condition that literature grapples with because few artists are willing to pay the price for a higher path to their true self; and it pained me to watch the brilliant young writer's anguished soul on *Charlie Rose*. He looked like he wanted to run away from himself, which every shadow-afflicted addict does; and David Foster Wallace was an addict.

On the other hand, after fifteen years of living hand-to-mouth on the bounty of a benevolent Universe, Jerry Wennstrom reconnected with his inner artist and went back to painting; and he wrote about his return to life in his memoir *The Inspired Heart—*

"However detached I may have become from the label 'artist,' I never lost sight of art's essential heartland, and I held a creative vision throughout my journey. My detachment from any particular religious affiliation did not preclude the essential spirituality of the journey. I hold true that the path lived attentively is a sacred path, and that the fundamental spirit of art is alive, well, and deeply esoteric. As does any spiritual path, art has the potential to deliver us into our own true *becoming*, which is identical to our world's becoming. Art expresses and defines the deep and collective spirit of our time."

Jerry Wennstrom realized that the *transcendent function* of his art could not satisfy the longing in his soul to *become* more, and he burnt all of his art and gave away his possessions and abandoned his life to God; and after fifteen years the triumphant hero returned to his art with an *enlightened attitude*, just as Katherine Mansfield would have done had she not died at such an early age; and just as David Foster Wallace could have done had he the wisdom to realize that his path had taken him as far as it could and that he needed a higher path to fulfill his enormous talent —which, according to his biographer D. T. Max (*Every Love Story Is A Ghost Story*), he had started looking for with his interest in Buddhism; but the call to a higher path was not strong enough to set him free from his tortured bifurcated self; and he never got to go on the hero's journey to his true self.

When Gurdjieff's system brought me to a dead end, I did not know where to turn; and I fell into deep despair. Then out of the blue the thought came to me: if I can't figure out which way to go, why not let God decide for me?

And I dared to "let go and let God" with the toss of a coin whenever I had a hard decision to make; that's how I lived my life for six months, risking my whole future to the toss of a coin. "Heads I do, tails I don't," I would say, but I had to be true to the toss for my experiment to be true; that's how I lost a possible romance with a beautiful young woman I had fallen for. But that was the point, and long before Jerry Wennstrom I trusted a higher good by "letting go and letting God."

But then something happened; something that I could not believe but had to: whenever my gut said yes to a decision, my coin affirmed my gut feeling; and whenever my gut said no to a decision, my coin affirmed my gut feeling. The odds of this happening every single time I tossed my coin boggled my mind. And I made the connection that whenever I "let go and let God" all I was doing was abandoning to my Higher Self—God in me, if you will; And I stopped "letting go and letting God" and trusted my own gut feelings, because I realized that whatever choice I made I was responsible for my own life—a lesson that over the period of twenty years gestated into the magical realism of my allegorical novel *The Golden Seed*.

With this reckless but richly rewarding experience, I realized that my own life was the path to my true self regardless of what teachings I studied; and despite how influenced I would be by every teaching that I explored, I knew that my own life was the way to the *pearl of great price*; and this gave me enormous freedom from the world.

Gurdjieff taught me how to "work" on myself, and the more I "worked" on myself the more I discerned the Way everywhere—in my work, in what people said and did, the books and magazines that I read, and TV shows and movies I watched, like a magic highlighter lighting up the Way for me in my daily life; which is why I eventually came to call the Way the omniscient guiding force of life.

But the word Way is a much simpler term to describe the self-transcending power of the creative life force, which I now *know* to be Divine Spirit and essential energy of God; and this is the energy of the *Creative Life Stream* that one taps into with their *transcendent function* that is responsible for what Updike called "creation's giddy bliss." And the more Updike wrote, the more he was himself. That's what made him such a prolific writer, because the need to be all that he could be possessed him to write to nourish his hungry soul; but not as much as it possessed me, because I went to extremes to *become* my true self.

I "worked" on myself with pathological commitment; but what made "working" on myself so effective was my private oath of silence. By not telling anyone what I was doing, I garnered more power from the creative life force that I needed to "create" my own soul; which, in reality, only nourished my inner self with the vital energy that I "swallowed" from my ego personality and shadow self. That's what it means to "work" on oneself. And I also "gathered and collected" more life force by simply being a good person, little realizing of course just how difficult it was be a good person in a world that's always out to compromise the very soul of who we are. And I wrote daily.

That's how I connected with the *Creative Life Stream* and came to see why writers have to write; because the act of writing is one of the most effective ways to tap into the creative energy of life and activate the *transcendent function* that individuates our inner and outer self into one harmonious unhypocritical self, which was why Hemingway loved writing more than anything else.

We *become* who we are meant to be and satisfy our greatest need in life by being creative, and a writer has to write and a painter has to paint and a musician has to play music and the workaholic has to work and so on because their own path *is* their way of *becoming* their true self. But, sadly, the way of life is not enough to satisfy the longing in our soul to *become* all that we are all meant to be; and that's the tragedy of all the arts and mystery of the human condition that was my calling to resolve…

10. *The Divine Plan of God*

The secret "it" is the magic ingredient of life, the inherently self-transcending power of our *becoming* and omniscient guiding force of life whose purpose is to create and sustain life and individuate the consciousness of God; and this is not theory or speculation with me: it's the gnostic truth of my own life experience…

I had an experience many years ago when I began "working" on myself with Gurdjieff's teaching that brought me back to the exact moment in time when life began on planet Earth, an experience that took me forty years to understand; but only because of my past-life regression to the Body of God that gave me the perspective to understand.

When I left university to forge my own path in life, I made a decision to build my life upon the truth of my own experiences; and truth by simple truth, I began to feel a little more secure in the same incomprehensible world that one of my favorite writers at university called "meaningless and absurd."

Making sense of life takes a long time, if ever at all as Albert Camus failed to do; but I was driven to know who and why I was, and I wasn't going to stop seeking until I found my true self. And as much as I loved Albert Camus at university, I had to walk on my own legs; and so I dropped out of academia for my own sanity.

"I give you good leather, but you must make your own shoes," said Gurdjieff, whose eclectic teaching I "chanced" upon at university in Ouspensky's book *In 'Search of the Miraculous*; and by "working" on myself with his system I made my own shoes that made walking through life feel safe, but unbelievably lonely.

I never told anyone about my experience of witnessing the genesis of life on planet Earth, because who would had believed me? Besides, I had no idea what it meant until forty years later when I connected the dots with my past-life regression to the Body of God where all souls come from; only then did my experience of going back in time to witness the genesis of life make sense to me.

It was a sunny spring day, and I was sitting in the back yard in a wind-sheltered corner of our family home soaking in the warm rays of the sun. It had been a long, hard winter, as they usually are in Northwestern, Ontario; and I took time off to sit in the back yard and soak in the warm sun before going back to work. I leaned my chair back and rested my head on the warm speckled green and white stucco of our family home, and I shut my eyes. The warm sun felt good on my face, and I let my mind drift; and that's when it happened.

I felt myself being pulled back through time, through the weeks and month and years, through the centuries, millennia, and eons, all the way back to when there was no life on planet Earth. I was too caught up in my time-travelling experience to question what was happening to me, and I just went with it.

I can't explain how I got there, but I was looking down on planet Earth; but it was not the luminous blue orb that Carl Jung saw when he left his body after his heart attack and looked down at the world from ten thousand miles above. The planet that I looked upon was dull and grey and completely barren of all life, with clouds of vaporous gases rising and mixing with the vaporous gases of the sky, and when they mixed they formed amino acids, the first building blocks of life; and then I felt myself slipping into the amino acids and ensoul them with the vital energy that initiated the process of life on planet Earth.

I experienced the birth of life itself when I ensouled the amino acids that created single-celled life forms that evolved through the multifarious stages of life on planet Earth, all the way up to one of the higher primate stages which I went back to in my past-life regression where I experienced the birth of my reflective self. This was why I could never make sense of my experience. I had to experience the birth of my reflective self first to connect the dots with my experience of the birth of life on planet Earth; only then could I see the big picture and solve the impenetrable riddle of life.

That *was* my experience, *my* truth; but it took many years to put it all together into what I came to call the Divine Plan of God; and I had to do a lot of creative writing to see that the fully self-realized "I" that ensouled the first building blocks of life in my experience back through time was the same un-self-realized "I" that activated the life process; and the "I" that activated the life process had to evolve through life to become the fully self-realized "I" that I am today. It boggled my mind; but when I experienced myself kick-starting the life process on planet Earth, I experienced myself before I *became* myself!

Finally, after years of puzzling what God said to Moses on Mount Sinai when he asked God for his name, I understood what God meant when he replied, "I AM THAT I AM." **THAT** is the operative word, because **THAT** speaks to the process of the un-self-realized "I" of God *becoming* a self-realized "I" of God. And I had to conclude that the un-self-realized "I" of God that initiated the life process had to be the I-consciousness of the vital life force that flows through all of life.

That's how I came to realize that the un-self-realized "I" of God was Soul and seed of our un-realized divine nature that had to evolve through life to grow in the consciousness of its own identity until it was evolved enough to take evolution into its own hands and realize what Jesus called the *pearl of great price*—our own divine self; and then like Jesus we could say, "I and my Father are One."

But it took me ten years after I wrote *Cathedral of My Past Lives* to realize that my experience of the birth of life on planet Earth, and the birth of my reflective self in my first primordial human lifetime, and the birth of my Higher Self in my mother's kitchen in my current life *were* the "Cathedral" of God's Divine Plan—the "house of worship" of God's sacred purpose of God *becoming* God!

Strangely enough, I did not choose the title of the novel I wrote on my past-life regressions; I was given that title by a friend with a psychic gift at one of our spiritual worship services in Orillia. To my surprise, she told me that she saw the cover of my unpublished book; and the title she saw was *Cathedral of My Past Lives.*

I loved the title, but I had no idea what it meant until ten years later when I connected the dots of the three births of Soul in the world—the birth of life, the birth of reflective self-consciousness, and the birth of spiritual self-realization consciousness, all of which I experienced in my long and lonely journey to the *pearl of great price*. Together the three births of Soul in life constitute the Divine Plan of God.

And that's how I came to see the distinction between Soul and Divine Spirit. Soul is the I-consciousness of Divine Spirit, and Spirit is the vital creative energy of God; and the purpose of life is to individuate the I-consciousness of God with the ensouling vital energy of God through karma and reincarnation until Soul has evolved enough self-identity to complete what Nature cannot finish.

That's how I confirmed with my own experience Wordsworth's insight that we all come from God, Keats's insight that we have to create our own individual identity, "a bliss peculiar to each one by individual existence," and Jean Houston's ironic insight that "the selfing game is what infinity does for fun." And whether we like it or not, we all have to play the "selfing game" until we win the ultimate prize—the *pearl of great price*. Only then does life make sense...

11. *The Way of Being and Non-being*

"As does any spiritual path, art has the potential to deliver us into our own true *becoming*, which is identical to our world's becoming. Art expresses and defines the deep and collective spirit of our time," wrote Jerry Wennstrom in *The Inspired Heart*; but art was not enough to deliver Jerry to his true self, and he abandoned the way of art in search of a higher path, which he found by abandoning his life to a "higher good" that was infinitely wiser than himself.

In his own words, he tells us that he had to drop his art to satisfy the unbearable longing in his soul: "As a spiritual path, art carried my life as far as it could within the limited scope of determined human effort and discipline. I knew that I could not have given one more ounce of myself to art as worship and have survived. In retrospect, I honestly believe that my survival was at stake—certainly survival of the spirit, perhaps of the body as well. Ramakrishna has a wonderful parable about the vehicle of one's particular discipline: When you take a boat across the river and you reach the other side, you do not drag the boat with you beyond that point."

Art had brought him across the river, and Jerry Wennstrom abandoned his art and trusted God to guide his way; and after fifteen years of living his new life he re-connected with his inner self on a deeper level and went back to painting. He was the same artist, but with an *enlightened attitude* that he had awakened to by trusting God, just as I had done with my bold experiment of "letting go and letting God."

As every path in life will do, Jerry Wennstrom's path had brought him to the realization that he needed a higher path to satisfy the longing in his soul to be all that he longed to be; and the higher path that he found by surrendering to the Universe was the *enlightened attitude* of the secret way that bridged the divide of his inner and outer life that satisfied his desperate longing to be more.

When he came back into the world with his *enlightened attitude*, Jerry Wennstrom was often asked by people what tradition he followed; and he replied in that mystical way that all initiates of the secret way do: "I listened for the moments when *that*, which contains the vastness of *everything*, specifically led me, one small and searching individual, somewhere in particular." And he added, with disarming humility, "Courage was all I knew to use as a guidepost."

Jerry Wennstrom found the secret way by trusting God to guide his life, but he couldn't explain it; the most that he could do was hint at it: "I continued to listen from within, learning to trust the ways of an unknown and formless spiritual path. I use the word *formless* loosely here. The path I followed had an unseen form. It could never have carried with it the progressive levels of understanding or the timely, saving moments of grace with their essential material gifts if it did not have its own vast, intelligent form. This fluid form was often terrifying to my small human mind, as it grappled with the all-inclusive expansiveness of infinite possibility." This is why I eventually came to call the secret way the omniscient guiding force of life, which when all is said and done is Divine Spirit.

And that's the tragedy of David Foster Wallace's life. His post-modern novel *Infinite Jest* (which Gurdjieff would have called "a pouring from the empty into the void") reflected the desperate longing in his soul and the tortured, conflicted spirit of our modern world; but in all of his literary genius, his writing wasn't enough to bridge the great divide of this fractured world and save his soul from his shadow-afflicted self; and out of desperation he killed himself.

David Foster Wallace's life begs the question that art cannot answer: what is this *enlightened attitude* that will bridge the great divide of our inner and outer self that Wallace so poignantly saw in the modern world and reflected in his writing, because despite his celebrated genius he couldn't find it?

This was my quest. I had to find a way to bridge the harrowing divide of my false shadow self and my true inner self, which I wrote about in *The Summoning of Noman* when I was called two years ago to study my dreams and Jung's psychology of individuation; and as abstruse as it may sound, the great divide that art cannot bridge is the paradoxical nature of our *being* and *non-being*.

David Foster Wallace couldn't bridge this gap, and neither could my literary mentor Ernest Hemingway; and that's what destroyed them. But Carl Gustav Jung bridged the gap between the *being* and *non-being* of his enantiodromiac self, and he went on to live a full and complete life; and all because he had cultivated the *enlightened attitude* of the secret way that resolved his two selves, just as the *enlightened* artist Jerry Wennstrom is doing so today.

Every path in life leads to the secret way, and the mystery of the secret way is an *enlightened attitude* which is always realized in an individual way—Wennstrom in his own way, Jung in his way, and I in mine; which makes the secret way an individual path. But however we come upon it, the *enlightened attitude* of our individual way resolves the paradoxical nature of our two selves and bridges the divide that keeps our *being* and *non-being* from becoming our transcendent self.

Our transcendent self is our true self, which Jesus called the *pearl of great price*; and despite what we have been told by the great religions of the world—Christianity, Judaism, Islam, Buddhism, and Hinduism; including the New Age Religion of the Light and Sound of God that claims to be "the most direct path to God"—we are not our true self until we *become* our true self. Otherwise, what is the purpose of life?

I wrote *The Summoning of Noman* because I wanted to make this point, using my own quest for my true self to state my case that there are two ways in life, the way of *being* and the way of *non-being*—the way of the world and the way of Spirit; and until we understand this dynamic of the natural process of individuation, we will never solve the mystery of our own identity.

In his quest for his lost soul, Carl Jung initiated himself into the secret way of life, which he chronicled in *The Red Book*; and he spent the rest of his life bridging the great divide of his Personality No. 1, and Personality No. 2—his *being* and *non-being*; and he was informed in a dream shortly before he died that he had transcended himself and achieved wholeness and singleness of self.

But what is this transcended self that Jesus called the *pearl of great price*? What kind of self is the integrated consciousness of our *being* and *non-being*? What is our resolved paradoxical self?

When I gave birth to my transcendent self that fine day in my mother's kitchen while she was kneading bread dough on the kitchen table, I *knew* that I was immortal and would never die. I had worked so hard to bridge the great divide of my *being* and *non-being* that I *became* my true self; and the only way I can describe the consciousness of my transcendent self would be in the language of philosophy: ***I am what I am not, and I am not what I am; I am both, but neither: I am Soul.***

This is the "Mystic Flower of the Soul" that Jung recognized in *The Secret of the Golden Flower*, the one united self of the alchemical marriage, the Self of the Sufi Path, and the *pearl of great price* of Christ's teaching of making the two into one; but whatever our transcendent self is called, it is what we are meant to be—"a bliss peculiar to each one by individual existence," our Soul Self.

12. *The Lure of Our Becoming*

"What is the soul?" Oprah Winfrey asked Jean Houston on Oprah's *Super Soul Sunday*; and Jean Houston, an initiate of the secret way, replied: *"I believe that the soul is the essence of who and what we are. I personally believe that it transcends our leaving this material world, and I think it is also in part that great friend that I talked about that comes with codes and possibilities and the next layers of who and what we may yet be; it is often a pain in the neck, because it says wake up, don't go to sleep, and I think it is also the lure of our becoming."*

"The lure of our becoming," Oprah repeated two or three times, with that wide-eyed look that all seekers of a higher path have when they "hear" the golden-tongued wisdom of the secret way speaking to them; and Oprah basked in the joy of feeling a little closer in her journey to the *pearl of great price*.

Long before I wrote *What Would I Say Today If I Were to Die Tomorrow?* I came to see that we will never make sense of life until we embrace the principle of reincarnation, and that every life we live is determined by our own karma; but it wasn't until I had seven past-life regressions many years later and caught a glimpse of the Divine Plan of God that I came to see that we have two destinies—one karmic and self-created, and one spiritual and ordained.

In my regression to the Body of God where all new souls come from, I learned that we are all atoms of God without identity, just as Keats saw with his poet's eye; and I learned in the same regression that we are sent into the world to evolve through life for the purpose of creating our own identity, a new "I" of God, which happened to me when I gave birth to my reflective self-consciousness in my first primordial human lifetime as the alpha male of a small group of ten or twelve higher primates; and life after life we grow in our own identity until we are evolved enough to take evolution into our own hands to satisfy that longing in our soul until we give birth to our eternal, spiritual self as I experienced one summer day while my mother was kneading bread dough on the kitchen table, thus completing my purpose in life; but what does the acorn seed do when it has become an oak tree?

The oak tree lives until it dies, giving back its essence to the life process in the acorn seeds it sheds from year to year; but it lives in the knowledge that it has fulfilled its purpose in life, which is what I replied to Penny one morning when she asked if I was happy with my life: "Given that I've achieved what I came into this life to achieve, yes; I would say I'm happy." I came to find my true self, which I did; and like the oak tree, I'm giving back my essence in each new book I write.

I always had the feeling growing up that I was going to be the last of my own line, but I had no idea what that meant until I found reincarnation; and when I had seven past-life regressions I learned why we have to keep coming back. But I finally broke the cycle of my karmic destiny and could say that I was happy. Which does not mean that I'm free of the bumps and grinds of daily life. It only means that I have satisfied the lure of my becoming and am no longer driven to *be* me. That's why I'm happy with my life. I'm free of the pull of my karmic destiny.

In her book *The Search for the Beloved*, Jean Houston offers the *enlightened* perspective that the deepest yearning in every human soul is to return to its spiritual source, which I can affirm with my experience of the Divine Plan of God; but how to satisfy our deepest yearning has puzzled the world since the dawn of man.

The strangest feeling came over me in my regression when I experienced the dawning of my reflective self-consciousness in my first primordial human lifetime; I felt frightened and alone, a feeling that I had never experienced before, like I had been separated from everything in my life. But more than feeling frightened and alone, I yearned. I could not fathom why I yearned, but my yearning was so great that it overrode my fear of being separate and alone, and I quickly lost my status as the alpha male and spent the rest of my life feeling cowered.

Of course, I didn't know why I yearned; I just yearned. And if I were to explain my yearning, it was like an empty, hollow need. And this, I believe, is the primal source of what Jean Houston has called the lure of our becoming. *We yearn to satisfy the empty, hollow need in our soul; and from lifetime to lifetime we seek out experiences that will satisfy our yearning for more identity.* This is what pulls us back into life, and we will keep coming back until we satisfy our yearning to be more ourselves; which can only be satisfied when we find the *pearl of great price*.

When I gave birth to my reflective self-consciousness I felt my separateness from all creation, because I was no longer one with the great unconscious soul of our becoming; and my separateness was responsible for my fear and loneliness, which I came to believe is the primal source of all our fears, especially when we are called to the hero's journey and have to break away from life and go it alone, as I had to do when I broke away from the three main paths of my life: my Roman Catholic faith, Gurdjieff's Work, and the New Age teaching of the Light and Sound of God that I embraced after Gurdjieff.

I dropped my Roman Catholic faith when I discovered reincarnation, but in all honesty the influence that my birth religion had upon me feels like a hangover that refuses to go away, and I've had to learn to live with the lingering effect of my youthful belief in mortal sin and eternal damnation, so it's difficult if not impossible to leave your boat behind once it has served its purpose of getting you to the other side; but dragging it with you only complicates your life, as it did mine when I refused to let go of my mentor Gurdjieff.

I needed help to let go, and I got it from one of my favorite students of Gurdjieff's teaching, who also happened to study with C. G, Jung before leaving Jung for Gurdjieff—Dr. Maurice Nicoll, who wrote *Psychological Commentaries on the Teaching of Gurdjieff and Ouspensky* among other books, my favorite being *The New Man: An Interpretation of Some Parables and Miracles of Christ.*

Doctor Nicoll came to me in a dream one night and told me that I had outgrown the Work and it was time to let Gurdjieff go, but I would not have embraced my new spiritual path had Dr. Nicoll not walked away also to embrace the same higher path that had come to me serendipitously when Gurdjieff's teaching had done all it could for me.

Still, it was hard letting go of Gurdjieff despite Dr. Nicoll's insistence, because Gurdjieff's system had awakened me to the secret way, and he had a special place in my heart.

And it was even harder to walk away from my New Age path thirty years later when it had served its purpose of widening my spiritual horizons; but I had to acknowledge the obdurate fact that every path is just another, albeit focused expression of the secret way, and that when all is said and done one's own life is the sum of all spiritual paths and *the* way to the Heart of God and Happiness. And so, with a heavy heart, I also thanked the New Age teaching that had brought me so much comfort, security, and wisdom and sadly said goodbye…

13. *Life Is Not a Useless Passion*

It took many years, but eventually I came to see that every path in life leads to the self and the secret way; and it took many more years to see that the mystery of the secret way is an *enlightened attitude,* which is always learned accordingly.

Which means that all paths lead to our divine self, and God; and no one path is more exclusive than another. Like spokes in a wheel, each path is as relevant as the other; and no one path is more right or better or more direct. But this only makes sense in light of the Divine Plan of God, because without the infinite mercy of the recurring cycle of life and death there would be no purpose to our existence. And yet, so many of us fall into such despair that we cannot see the purpose of our life. Shakespeare, better than any other writer, expresses this morbid feeling of tired dread with eloquent ease in his play *Macbeth*:

Tomorrow, and tomorrow, and tomorrow,
Creeps in this petty pace from day to day
To the last syllable of recorded time,
And all our yesterdays have lighted fools
The way to dusty death. Out, out, brief candle!
Life's but a walking shadow, a poor player
That struts and frets his hour upon the stage
And then is heard no more. It is a tale
Told by an idiot, full of sound and fury,
Signifying nothing.

When I went to France to find my true self, I poured myself into my first creative effort that I titled *This Petty Pace*; but as trapped as I was by my own despair, I just couldn't be swallowed whole by the demon beast of meaninglessness and absurdity. There was meaning to life. I knew it in my gut, but it wasn't my truth until it *became* my truth; that's why I was called to the hero's journey: I had to know.

But why the disparity? How could I on the one hand be drowning in such deep despair that Macbeth's words resonated with me completely while on the other hand I knew in my gut that he was wrong about life? Why the paradox?

This is the central mystery of human nature, the *being* and *non-being* of our *becoming*; and not until we resolve this paradox will we understand how we can be two selves in one body. This is where the hero's journey begins—in the depths of one's own soul where our two selves exist interchangeably.

One moment we are real, genuine, and happy; and the next moment we are false, disingenuous, and miserable. Why? And if that's not bad enough, if we are disingenuous enough we will one day be swallowed whole by our false self and won't even know that our entire life has become an elaborate, complex lie; and then we become one of those people that Dr. Scott Peck, author of *The Road Less Travelled* that helped launch the self-help movement, called "people of the lie."

I was one of those people and didn't know it; but I began to sense it in high school, and it tormented me night and day that I could be so false. That's why I became obsessed with the authentic/inauthentic dynamic that Jean-Paul Sartre explored in his philosophy. *"I am what I am not, and I am not what I am,"* said the existentialist philosopher, who did not believe in God; but he could not resolve the paradox of man's nature and was forced by the logic of his dialectic to conclude that "life is a useless passion."

But within the context of man's "useless" life, Sartre endowed man with meaning by acknowledging his freedom to choose; and he could choose to live his life in good or bad faith. If man chose to live his life in good faith, he was authentic; and if he chose to live his life in bad faith, he was inauthentic. And in this existential paradigm, Sartre concluded: *"Man is condemned to be free."*

Again, Sartre's conclusion about man's freedom to choose his life is born of his paradoxical nature, which Sartre could not resolve (*"I am what I am not, and I am not what I am"*), which dialectically forced him to conclude that man was condemned to be free; but what if man could resolve his paradoxical nature? Would he still be condemned to be free, or would he be free to be condemned?

Sartre saw no way out of the paradox of man's nature; but even if this did make intellectual sense to me, which it did, on a gut level I could not accept his philosophical conclusion.

This was another reason I left university to search for a higher path that would free me from myself; and I thank my lucky stars that the merciful law of synchronicity brought Gurdjieff into my life in my second year of studies, or I would still be out there floundering in that sea of endless philosophical speculation.

I vowed to find my true self or die trying, and philosophy had taken me as far as it could; and so, by the conatus of my own inner imperative I had to continue on my own with nothing but raw courage and Gurdjieff's spellbinding but indigestible teaching to guide me…

While studying Jung again for my book *The Summoning of Noman* I came to see something that I knew all along but refused to acknowledge, that we only have one self that is split in two, which Jung called Personality No. 1, and Personality No. 2; and the hero's journey, no matter which culture or time in history, has always been to resolve this split in our soul to fulfill our destined purpose in life.

Tired from a long day's work in my pool hall business in my hometown of Nipigon, Ontario when my hero's journey began, I became possessed one night by a sexual need that blocked out all judgement, a need so overpowering that it forced me to satisfy myself with no mind for the consequences; but after the deed was done and my sexual need satisfied sanity returned, and guilt possessed me.

Enormous, soul-crushing guilt; and like my namesake in Aeschylus's *Oresteia* who murdered his mother to avenge his father's murder, I also became haunted by my Furies for my unspeakable sin; and out of shame and self-revulsion I sold my investment in the pool hall business and fled to Annecy, France to begin my quest for my true self, because I knew that the person who did what he did that night was me but not me; and I had to solve the mystery of this other me.

Who was this creature that possessed me? I knew instinctively that it was me, but it was another me that I did not know existed; and only after I discovered Jung did I learn that it was my archetypal shadow self that had first erupted with daemonic fury out of the depths of my unconscious in my high school poem *Noman* that left me dazed and shocked my English teacher; and it came out again with ravenous sexual lust the night it took over my body like it was its own, and I had no control over myself. And I didn't go to France because I wanted to be like my romantic high school hero and literary mentor Ernest Hemingway, as I told everyone; I fled to France out of shame and guilt, and I could not get away fast enough.

Unfortunately, I don't have a copy of my narrative poem *Noman*, and all I remember are the last two lines which opened a window onto the mystery of the archetypal shadow self of man; but so powerful are those lines that whenever I think of them I feel the horror of my banishment from the God.

I explored my banishment from God in my spiritual memoir *The Summoning of Noman*, so suffice to say that my high school poem *Noman* foreshadowed the hero's journey that I was forced to make out of shame and guilt for my sexual indiscretion.

Noman, who in my poem is the archetypal shadow self of Everyman, is summoned to God for a reckoning; but Noman does not have the "fish's scale" (which I eventually deciphered to be my soul) that God has asked of him, and after three unsuccessful attempts to find his lost soul God condemns Noman to the "fourth corner of the abyss" to find it, and as he falls from Heaven Noman shouts with an injured sense of merit equal to Milton's Fallen Angel in *Paradise Lost*—

"Open you vile, voracious, loveable sweet whore!
God, why hast thou forsaken me?"

How is it possible for a teenage virgin to write those lines? Where did that passion come from? Why would Noman call life a "vile, voracious, loveable sweet whore"? And did God really forsake Noman, whom I knew instinctively as I wrote my poem was me? And why did this poem erupt out of me unannounced? Was it set free by the anonymous mystery play *Everyman* that I had read the week before?

Not long after I wrote *Noman,* I began having what I later came to learn were past-life recollection dreams; but it was only after I found my lost soul that I pieced together the puzzle of my poem *Noman.*

All the pieces finally fit, and the puzzle made sense to me: with every life we live, we create a new personality; this is the natural process of individuation that repeats itself every time we take on a new life. But every time we create a new personality, we create a shadow self as well; and when we die we take our personality and shadow self with us because they are who we are *becoming.* And we continue the process of creating a new personality and shadow self with each new life we live, until we have realized enough self-identity to be called to our true self, as I was with the eruption of my poem *Noman* in high school when God called me for a reckoning.

My soul belonged to God, and God wanted—nay, demanded it back; but I had lost my soul somewhere in the world, which in my poem is symbolized by "the four corners of the abyss." I was given three chances by God to find it, but I failed each time; and God condemned me to the "fourth corner of the abyss" to look for it.

This was my spiritual destiny, which I completed in my current lifetime; and having found my lost soul in the depths of my archetypal shadow self—which inspired the most agonized aphorism of my life, "**The shortest way to God is through hell***,* " I can safely say that Sartre was wrong: life is not a useless passion, because all of our passion, however meaningless and absurd it may appear to be, goes into the process of our own *becoming*; and the goal of our *becoming* is to create the most precious treasure in the world—*the pearl of great price!*

14. *Our Two Destinies*

We have two destinies: one spiritual, and pre-scripted; and the other karmic, and self-scripted. And not until we align our two destinies will we find *the pearl of great price*. This is the mystery of our *becoming*.

We create karma with every life we live, which necessitates the individuation process of our *becoming* through the inevitable karmic resolution of daily living; and not until we are evolved enough to realize that we are the authors of our own karmic destiny will we be called to align our karmic destiny with our pre-scripted spiritual destiny, as Jung was called to do when he realised that he had forfeited his soul for "honor, power, wealth, knowledge, and every human happiness." This was his *metanoic* change of heart, and the call to his spiritual destiny…

"Switzerland. Carl Gustav Jung. Born in 1875, with Freud, one of the founding fathers of modern psychology, still working at 84, he is the most honored living psychiatrist, and history will record him as one of the greatest physicians of all time," said John Freeman on the BBC program *Face to Face*, which was filmed at Jung's home in Kusnacht on the shores of Lake Zurich and broadcast to the world on *October 22, 1959*, introducing Jung to a wider public; and the response he got from this interview inspired—nay, demanded, because Jung never wrote a book until he was called to do so; and a dream he had led to *Man and His Symbols*, which he wrote with his close associates Marie-Louise von Franz, Joseph L. Henderson, Aniela Jaffe, and Jolande Jacobi, a book that introduced the general reader to the collective unconscious and the secret way of life in the "individuation process."

As Jung tells us in his commentary to *The Secret of the Golden Flower*, the technique that he developed in his practice of psychiatry and psychotherapy had unconsciously led him along the secret way, a healing modality which evolved into what he came to call "the process of individuation." Jung discerned the secret way in his work, and the more conscious he became of the secret way the more he embraced it in his life; that's how he resolved the paradox of his two selves.

But Jung came by the hidden knowledge of the secret way by choosing to take the way of the world, which cost him his soul; because by the age of forty he had achieved everything he had wished for himself and his desire for more success abated, and the horror of what it had cost him for his achievements compelled him to retrieve the soul he had forfeited for his success. That's when Jung was called to the hero's journey, which he chronicled in *The Red Book*.

"Do you remember the occasion when you first felt consciousness of your own individual self?" Freeman asked Jung.

Jung leaned forward, and with a twinkle in his eye and the sweetest trace of a smile on his octogenarian face, he took his pipe out of his mouth, and said: *"That was in my eleventh year. There I certainly, on my way to school, I stepped out of a mist. It was just as if I had been in a mist, walking in a mist, and I stepped out of it and I knew I am. I am what I am. And then I thought, but what have I been before? And then I found that I had been in a mist, not knowing to differentiate myself from things. I was just one thing among many things."*

Albert Camus would have called Jung's momentous experience a *"prise de conscience,"* a realization, or moment of consciousness; but Jung described it as a "sudden coming to consciousness," which suggests a numinous experience of his own autonomous *being*. And this is the mystery of Jung's own individuation, because he began his journey through life centered in his *being*, which he called his Personality No. 2; but to achieve the success he wished for in life, he had to develop his outer self, his Personality No. 1, which he did magnificently as he poured himself into his life's work. But it cost him his soul.

This is meant figuratively, of course; because no-one can ever lose their soul. Soul is who we are, the very essence of our *being* and *non-being*; and losing one's soul simply means that one has shifted their center of gravity (the "I" of their autonomous soul) from their *being* to their *non-being*—or, as Jung would say, from their inner self to their outer self—from Personality No. 2 to Personality No. 1. But to achieve success in the fledgling new science of psychotherapy, Jung had to grow in the ways of the world; which meant pouring his best energies into his outer self. That's how he shifted his center of gravity from his *being* to *non-being*; until the burden of his successful *non-being* Personality No. 1 became too much to bear.

"My soul, where are you? Do you hear me? I speak, I call you—are you there?" he asks in *The Red Book*, thus beginning his quest for the soul he had forfeited to his Personality No. 1—the same forfeiture that countless souls had made before him and will continue to make because this is how life works; and Jung spent the rest of his life integrating his inner and outer self until he found *the pearl of great price* in the wholeness and singleness of one self, as his own unconscious informed him in a dream just before passing over to the other side.

This was the premise of my memoir *The Lion that Swallowed Hemingway*; I wanted to illustrate the natural process of individuation with the life of these two vastly different men, how one got swallowed by his own shadow and died a tragic death, and the other who swallowed his own shadow and died happily resolved.

In *Meeting the Shadow, The Hidden Power of the Dark Side of Human Nature*, the editors Connie Zweig and Jeremiah Abrams wrote something that sheds light on the dark side of our personality: "We all have a shadow. Or does our shadow have us? Carl Jung turned this question into a riddle when he asked: *'How do you find a lion that has swallowed you?'* Because the shadow is by definition unconscious, and it is not always possible to know whether or not we are under the sway of some compelling part of the shadow's content."

Hemingway's dream in life was to become the best writer of his generation, and it could be argued that he accomplished his goal, given that he created a new style of writing that garnered him the Nobel Prize for Literature in 1954; but the price he paid for his success—all the betrayals, self-betrayals, and hurt and pain that he caused everyone who came into his life—was too much to bear; and in his memoir *A Moveable Feast* that he was working on before taking his own life, he confessed his remorse for going down the path he did, which began with the betrayal of his first wife Hadley Richardson: "When I saw my wife again standing by the tracks as the train came by the piled logs at the station, I wish I had died before I loved anyone but her." The great writer was remorseful, and he admits to himself and the world in his unforgiving memoir that the price of his success wasn't worth the love he lost when he betrayed his first wife, and he would have given it all up to reclaim the day he betrayed Hadley; but he couldn't reclaim his life, and he took out his favorite shotgun and killed himself.

Ernest Hemingway, my high school hero and literary mentor, whom I loved as a writer for the artistic integrity of his writing and grew to hate as a man for his ravenous self-serving ego, had a change of heart at the end of his broken, life-weary life; but it was too late to redeem his lost soul, and out of desperation took his own life.

But that was Ernest Hemingway. He always had to have life on his own selfish terms, including his own death; and that was the tragic flaw of his character that kept his two selves apart. It fueled his art, but it destroyed the man; and that's the way it was.

15. *Bridging the Great Divide*

"The struggle itself towards the heights is enough to fill a man's heart. One must imagine Sisyphus happy," said Albert Camus, who appropriated the ancient Greek myth of Sisyphus to illustrate the hopeless drudgery of daily life; but I could never imagine Sisyphus happy. I just couldn't. Our life was not vain and absurd; there had to be a purpose for all our labour. There had to be.

Sisyphus was condemned to Hades for offending the gods. His fate was to roll a boulder to the top of a hill whence it would roll back down of its own accord and he would have to roll it back up again, and again, and again forever; that was his fate.

That's how Camus saw life: a Sisyphean struggle. We have to struggle with the forces of life every single day, a never-ending toil; but is this the case? Many people think so, and they embrace Camus' philosophy of the absurdity of life; but this gloomy philosophy falls apart in light of our two destinies.

Before I chanced upon Gurdjieff's teaching in Ouspensky's book at university (by chance, I mean providentially granted), I was hampered by the philosophical constraints of the generally accepted belief that we only live one life; and despite the fact that Gurdjieff believed that not everyone was born with an immortal soul, they could create their own soul if they knew how, and they would be born again in another life to continue evolution to a higher state. That's why I was fascinated with Gurdjieff's teaching; it gave me hope.

Gurdjieff spoke to me on a level I could not explain, and despite how frustrating it was to make sense of his teaching I *had* to read everything I could find on this mysterious man; which led me to the publisher *Samuel Weiser* in New York City, and I ordered book after book on Gurdjieff and his teaching written by some of his most devoted students, many of whom were writers in their own right, and the more I read the closer I felt to a secret society of sacred wisdom. And then one night I met Gurdjieff in a dream, and he accepted me into his inner circle of students; that's why Gurdjieff was so special to me.

But I would never have broken the code of Gurdjieff's teaching had I not created my *Royal Dictum*, my edict of self-denial which gave me an entry point into Gurdjieff's transformative techniques of *non-identifying, self-remembering, voluntary effort,* and *conscious suffering*—all the tools that I needed to initiate myself into the secret way, and day by day the secret way revealed itself to me.

It's next to impossible to define the secret way, and every initiate will describe it in the language of their own path; but despite how difficult it is to put to words, the effect that the secret way has upon every initiate is to imbue them with that mysterious quality of gnostic *knowing*—an innate understanding of life's purpose and meaning; a sacred knowledge beyond the ken of human thought.

The artist Jerry Wennstrom awakened to the secret way when he abandoned his life to God, and he called it "an unknown and formless spiritual path." And the more he was guided by the secret way, the more he saw that it was a "vast, intelligent form with the all-inclusive expansiveness of infinite possibility," which he trusted implicitly until he bridged the chasm of his two selves and was ready to step back into life and take up his art again with an *enlightened attitude* that, as Wordsworth described in his poem *Character of the Happy Warrior*, "makes the path before him always bright"—bright with meaning and purpose, that is.

Jerry Wennstrom is a *knower* today. He *knows* the meaning and purpose of life implicitly because he has bridged the great divide of his two selves, and he reflects this sacred knowledge in his life, his manner, and his art—as does every initiate of the secret way reflect the sacred knowledge in who they are and what they do. This is why the secret way has to be an individual path, because only by bridging the great divide of our two selves will we find *the pearl of great price.*

When Gurdjieff said that we have to take evolution into our own hands because Nature can only evolve us so far, he *knew* that to "create" our own soul—which, in light of my understanding simply means bridging the chasm of our two selves—we have to make indefatigable conscious effort; and by conscious effort Gurdjieff meant taking evolution into our own hands.

This is why Gurdjieff called his teaching "work on oneself," because we cannot bridge the chasm of our two selves without "working" on all those aspects of our outer self that keep us from realizing our inner self. And the more we transform the consciousness of our outer self, the more we align our karmic destiny with our spiritual destiny—until they become one destiny, one path.

Carl Jung was also a *knower,* and he made it his life's mission to make conscious through his writing the sacred knowledge of the secret way of life; and when he said—to the chagrin of all his followers—"Thank God I'm Jung and not a Jungian," he was letting the world know that the way to one's true self is through one's own self.

This is why no one person, teaching, or religion can claim rights to the secret way, because the secret way cannot be possessed; on the contrary, one has be possessed by the secret way to bridge the chasm of their two selves. And there's only one way to be possessed by the secret way, and that's to *live* the imperative of the secret way.

This is the paradox of Christ's teaching: *"He that loveth his life shall lose it; and he that hateth his life in this world shall keep it unto life eternal."* Which was Christ's metaphorical way of saying that we have to transform the consciousness of our outer self to realize our eternal life, which he called *the pearl of great price.*

I learned to "die" to my outer life with my *Royal Dictum,* and the more I "died" to my outer life the more I bridged the chasm of my two selves. In effect, like Jesus said, by integrating the consciousness of my inner and outer selves I built my house upon a rock: *"Therefore whosoever heareth these sayings of mine, and doeth them, I will liken him unto a wise man, which built his house upon a rock. And the rain descended, and the floods came, and the winds blew, and beat upon that house; and it fell not: for it was founded upon a rock."*

This was how I initiated myself into the secret way and cultivated the *enlightened attitude* of my own path; but does one have to go to such extremes to bridge the great divide of their life?

Gurdjieff thought so, and so does an un-enlightened understanding of Christ's teaching; because if we take Christ's teaching literally, as Christianity does, we only have one life to live, and the only way to save our life is to embrace Jesus Christ as our personal savior—a concept that makes no sense in the Divine Plan of God, because no-one can short-circuit their own *becoming*; a realization that I distilled into one of my most prescient gnostic sayings: "**The only way out of life is through life**."

Thank God for the merciful law of reincarnation, then; because, as the old saying goes, "If we don't get it right in this lifetime, we will just keep coming back until we do." And getting it right means creating the right kind of personality that will bridge the great divide of our inner and outer life.

Again, that's how we find *the pearl of great price*.

16. *Follow Life and the Living*

In the Gospel of Matthew, Jesus said: *"Neither do men put new wine into old bottles, else the bottles break, and the wine runneth out, and the bottles perish; but they put new wine into new bottles, and both are preserved."* And two thousand years later, Jesus reiterates the same message to Glenda Green in her book *Love without End, Jesus Speaks*, but without metaphor: *"As we follow life and the living, we move forward. Life is being created anew each day, and consciousness is expanding with every new burst of life…"*

In an interview on *The Paul Holdengraber Show*, talking about her bestselling memoir *Eat, Pray, Love*, subtitled *One Woman's Search for Everything Across Italy, India, and Indonesia*, that had just been released by Hollywood in a movie by the same name starring Julia Roberts, Elizabeth Gilbert quoted her mother on the counsel that she gave her when she was fifteen or sixteen years old. "You know, there are decisions you are going to have to make in your life that nobody can make for you," and then Elizabeth, being the gifted writer that she is, distilled the rest of her mother's sage advice into a precious little gem of aphoristic wisdom that speaks to the secret way: **"Life is a journey that nobody can take for you and nobody can spare you from,"** sacred knowledge that speaks to the uniqueness of every person's passage through life—which is why writers write stories.

Stories are the bearers of the meaning and purpose of life, and every person's story is original despite how familiar it may appear to be; and the originality of every person's story lies in the relationship of one's two selves. Insomuch that we are all pre-scripted to realize our divine nature, we are all the same; but no two people have the same karmic destiny, and this makes every person's story special.

Somerset Maugham once said that he could talk to a person for an hour and have a story, but the lure of every person's story is that it can never be brought to resolution because our life is incomplete until we complete what Nature cannot finish, which we cannot do without the sacred knowledge of the secret way.

This is why writers *have* to write: they want to find an answer to the meaning and purpose of life, vainly hoping that if they dig deep enough with their art they will find it in their stories. And they write and write in passionate unawareness until one day they throw their hands into the air and like the frustrated Updike declare all writing to be a "faint thread excreted out of ourselves."

This is why Katherine Mansfield, whose short stories Hemingway cruelly called "near-beer," said that literature wasn't enough; there had to be more to life than literature could unearth, and she went in search of a higher path which she found in Gurdjieff's teaching. But one does not have to go on a spiritual quest to the far corners of the world like Elizabeth Gilbert did to find the meaning and purpose of their life, because the secret way is everywhere to be found.

Carl Jung found it. Jerry Wennstrom found it. William Wordsworth found it, which he shared with the world in his magnificent poem *Character of the Happy Warrior*; and I found it also in the backwoods of Northwestern Ontario. But why? What did we have that led us to the secret way of life?

DESPERATION. That's what we had. Life had brought us as far as it could, and we were desperate to satisfy the longing in our soul to be more. Jung was desperate to find his lost soul; Jerry Wennstrom was desperate to satisfy the longing that his art no longer gave him; and I was desperate to find my true self. Like every person that life brings to the limits of natural evolution, we were desperate to satisfy the longing in our soul that life could no longer give us; and we dared to risk it all to satisfy the unbearable longing to be more. We had no choice.

As long as we have a choice in our life, the secret way will never reveal itself to us; because the paradoxical mystery of the secret way is that we have to surrender to the great unknown to satisfy the longing in our soul for our true self, which Jesus so beautifully called *the pearl of great price,* just as my friend Alice was called to find and pay for with her mortal life as Jesus promised with his most sacred parable.

    The Jesus in Glenda Green's astonishing memoir *Love without End, Jesus Speaks* is the same Jesus of the New Testament Gospels, the same Jesus who came into the world from another time to share with us the secret way, but with one distinct difference: the Jesus in Glenda's book is Jesus without metaphor, and what he told Glenda in their casual conversations while she painted his portrait is nothing less than the sacred knowledge of the secret way that he could not reveal to the public during his short mission on Earth, because the public was not ready to hear the simple truth of the secret way but is ready to hear today; which is why he said to Glenda—

    "***Simply follow life and the living!*** *The whole universe is built around a priority for life and the living. Therefore you cannot afford to ignore this principle. Do not follow the dead and dying. By this I mean do not adapt to ways of life, structures, ideas, concepts, or businesses which are becoming ineffective and obsolete. Look for new alignments, opportunities, and understandings which refresh your life, Our Father created this universe to celebrate life and to go on forever. In order to ensure this would always be true, He gave priority to the living…If you want to be successful, give your full and uncompromised support to life and the living. As you follow life and the living, you will instinctively do the right thing. When you do the right thing, you are being the love that you are.*"

    I know I'm doing the right thing when I'm blessed with the sanctifying grace of little coincidences throughout the day, because coincidences tell me that I'm in sync with life; which means that my life is in harmony with the *Creative Life Stream* that is forever flowing into the Heart of God and Happiness; like the surprising little coincidence I was blessed with when I drove into Midland yesterday morning to pick up my weekend papers and list of groceries that Penny had given me.

    I had done my writing for the day, stopping with what Jesus had told Glenda about following life and the living, and as I drove into Midland I was thinking about how stories bear he meaning and purpose of life and how they reflect the truth of their time and place in history; and I also thought of what Jesus said about consciousness being expanded with each new burst of life, which was why he wanted us to follow life and the living and not the dead and dying, and suddenly it occurred to me just how valuable contemporary stories are because they bear the meaning and purpose of life in our time, hot off the press as it were; but I didn't know how I was going to convey that sacred knowledge when suddenly I heard Terry O'Reilly, host of the show THE AGE OF PURSUASION, say on the radio, **"the guidance and understanding that stories give us…"**

    I've experienced coincidences like this many times in my life, especially when I'm working on another book; and every time they speak to me I feel a wave of goodness wash over me, like I've just been blessed with the sanctifying grace of Holy Spirit, and I always feel a little better, a little holier—which was what St. Padre Pio meant when he told me in my seventh spiritual healing session with the gifted psychic who channeled him for my novel *Healing with Padre Pio*—"He said again, watch the synchronicities, the coincidences, because they will bring you goodness. So pay attention to goodness; goodness in others, goodness around you; pay attention to goodness." And the goodness of my coincidence on the road to Midland confirmed that today's writers are the bearers of today's wisdom; and reading today's writers would be following life and the living, just as Jesus admonished two thousand years ago to put new wine into new bottles…

17. *The Wonder of Story*

"The guidance and understanding that stories give us," was what I heard on the radio as I pondered the question of how to make my point on how stories convey the meaning and purpose of life, an answer provided by the omniscient guiding force of life that Jerry Wennstrom called "an unknown and formless spiritual path" which I had to take seriously because it was infinitely wiser than me; and on the rest of my drive to Midland I pondered the deeper meaning of my timely coincidence, because I knew that it was an entry point to the wonder of story that I had been guided to explore with my study of the gifted scholar and champion of the western canon of literature, the inimitable Professor Harold Bloom of Yale University.

It never fails when I'm writing a new book, I'm *pulled* to authors that I have to read for the sake of my story; but I never see their relevance to the theme of my story until I get to that part of my story that calls for the authors that I had been called to read—contemporary authors like Elizabeth Gilbert, Ann Patchett, Barbara Kingslover, and Martin Amis, to name only a few; and so I went online and watched all the interviews on You Tube that I could find on these contemporary authors to begin my study, and I became fascinated by the phenomenally erudite professor with the "scandalous memory" who in his thirties read one thousand pages an hour and continues to read in his venerable eighties at a pace that he still calls "freakish."

But the more I studied the great scholar, who soared above the clouds when he talked about his favorite writers, especially Whitman Shakespeare, and Ralph Waldo Emerson, he could not quite put his finger on the central mystery of story. He alludes to the mystery by calling it "wisdom writing" and "the tradition of literature," which he corralled in his compendium classic *The Western Canon*; but as to what the mystery of story was, he could not say, and that's what the genius of my little coincidence on the road to Midland opened up to me—**"the guidance and understanding that stories give us."**

But what is this mysterious "it" that transforms reality into a greater perception of what is, the same mysterious "it" that Updike recognized in "creation's giddy bliss" which my mentor Hemingway called "the secret that is poetry" and Professor Bloom acknowledges as the wisdom that flows through all great literature but cannot define? What is this connective tissue that speaks from the soul of the writer directly to the soul of the reader? What is this "omniscient voice" that gives us guidance and understanding for our journey through life?

Every reader recognizes "it" when a story speaks to them, but they can't define what "it" is; the most they can say is that the story spoke to them. But what did the story "say" that they "heard"? That's the wonder of story.

In one of my spiritual healing sessions with the gifted psychic that inspired *Healing with Padre Pio*, the Good Saint said two things that speak to the wonder of story: "Life is a journey of the self," and "life is all about growth and understanding." I understood what he meant, because I had been initiated into the mystery of the self from its origin in the Body of God to its inception in the life process and as far as Nature could take me, and then to the wholeness and singleness of my true self; so I had no comment to make other than my appreciation for his confirmation of my own experience. But herein lies the mystery of "it" and the wonder of story.

"It" is the connective tissue of all great literature, the Ariadne's string that leads us out of the darkness of our *non-being* into the light of growth and understanding of our *being* and transcendent Self, the message that satisfies our longing to know the way out of our problems and dilemmas; this is why Jesus counselled Glenda to follow life and the living, because it takes a living author to address the problems and dilemmas of today's world, an author who can tap into the *Creative Life Stream* and imbue his stories with timely wisdom just as I experienced on the road to Midland when "it" provided the answer to my quandary on how to best convey the wonder of story. It may not have been as dramatic as St. Paul's epiphany on the road to Damascus; but it was what I needed, which is precisely what Jesus meant by following life and the living. "It" pointed me to contemporary writers!

"It" is the omniscient guiding force of life; the "unknown and formless spiritual path" that is the ground of our *being* and *non-being*. "It" is the guiding voice of life that speaks to us in our time of need. "It" is what Emerson called "God within," and writers that connect with the *Creative Life Stream* tap into the eternal wisdom of "it" and grace their stories with the sacred knowledge that readers need to satisfy their longing to understand their reason for being.

"As far as we can discern, the sole purpose of human existence is to kindle a light in the darkness of mere being," said Carl Jung in his historic memoir *Memories, Dreams, Reflection*s; and stories shed light into the darkness of our *being* and *non-being* so we can grow in our understanding of life. But, sadly, as Katherine Mansfield realized, literature cannot give us what we need to satisfy the longing in our soul to be all that we are meant to be; the most that story can do is help us to cultivate an *enlightened attitude* that will open us up to the secret way which will take us, if we have the courage and wisdom to follow our path, to the transcendent Self of *the pearl of great price*. This is our reason for being, and the wonder of story…

18. *The Dust on a Butterfly's Wings*

In his melancholic memoir *A Moveable Feast*, the last book he was working on before taking his own life, Hemingway said something about his friend and writer F. Scott Fitzgerald, who had introduced the young Hemingway to his legendary editor Maxwell Perkins at *Scribner's* who helped launch Hemingway's career, that alcohol had ruined Fitzgerald's precious talent—

"His talent was as natural as the pattern that was made by the dust on a butterfly's wings. At one time he understood it no more than the butterfly did and he did not know when it was brushed or marred. Later he became conscious of his damaged wings and of their construction and he learned to think and could not fly anymore because the love of flight was gone and he could only remember when it had been effortless."

My literary mentor learned the hard way that imagination was vital to giving story wings when he boldly "attempted to write an absolutely true book to see whether the shape of a country and the pattern of a month's action can, if truly presented, compete with a work of imagination," which his novel *Green Hills of Africa* failed to do miserably, and Hemingway never did that again.

"It" is the dust on a butterfly's wings, the secret that makes good writing take flight. In a letter to Harvey Breit, dated 1952, Hemingway wrote: "In truly good writing no matter how many times you read it you do not know how it is done. That is because there is a mystery in all great writing and the mystery does not dis-sect out. It continues and it is always valid. Each time you re-read it you see or learn something new." This is the mystery of "it", the dust on a butterfly's wings, the eternal wisdom that writers tap into when they let imagination transform reality into a deeper perception of what is, and each time we read a great story we are let into the secret mystery and learn something new.

This something new is the perennial wisdom that's passed on in literature, **"the guidance and understanding that stories give us"** to satisfy the longing in our soul to be all that we are meant to be, which Professor Bloom preserved and defended in *The Western Cannon* and many of his other books, all championing the cause of literature despite literature's inability to resolve the basic issue of the human condition; and of all the writers that I have read, Professor Bloom comes closest to ferreting out the secret way that literature struggles to reveal.

Gurdjieff had a powerful saying that speaks to the basic nature of the human condition, a saying that reflected his mystic philosophy which he said was drawn from the hermetic tradition of "esoteric Christianity," a saying no less cryptic than any of Christ's sayings which, in the words of Professor Bloom, inflicted an "immortal wound" upon me: **"Happy is the man who has a chair to sit on, unhappy is the man who has no chair to sit on; but woe to the man who stands between two chairs."** The lance of truth pierced my soul, and I bled.

I stood between two chairs. I knew this on such a deep level that I *had* to follow Gurdjieff's teaching to save myself, and I became pathological in my commitment to have a chair to sit on, which I finally did one day in my mother's kitchen while she was kneading bread dough on the kitchen table; but not my literary mentor.

Ernest Hemingway died miserably torn between two chairs, which I expound upon in *The Lion that Swallowed Hemingway*. That's why Hemingway spoke to me: he reflected the state of his miserable condition, which he captured with poetic genius in his short story "A Clean, Well-lighted Place."

By chair, Gurdjieff meant soul; and given his philosophical premise, one who has an immortal soul is happy and one who doesn't is unhappy, but one who is in the process of creating their own soul is miserable. This is the basic state of the human condition; but it took me years to solve the enantiodromiac riddle of man's *being* and *non-being*, and when I did literature finally made sense to me.

"There is nothing but the self and God," said Jesus to Glenda Green in her book *The Keys of Jeshua*, which I *know* to be true in that

mystic gnostic way that can never be proven; but provable or not, it resolves the mystery of the human condition that literature has grappled with since the dawn of story-telling.

Stories bear the truth of the human condition, and the human condition is the story of our *becoming*; but not until we solve the riddle of our *becoming* will literature resolve the issue of the human condition. This makes literature endlessly fascinating, because every writer speaks to their place in the enantiodromiac process of man's *becoming*, which Jung called "individuation," and in their stories they stake out the geography of man's soul—whether it be the happy country of one's *being*, the unhappy country of one's *non-being*, or that miserable place of being stuck between two countries—the no-man's land of one's soul.

I was stuck in the no-man's land of my soul, which was revealed to me with daemonic ferocity in my high school poem *Noman*; and my destiny was to go on a quest for my lost soul in the country of my *non-being*. And once I traversed the no- man's land of my soul with Gurdjieff's teaching and my *Royal Dictum*, I resolved the basic issue of the human condition; that's why I wrote about my heroes Hemingway and Jung in *The Lion that Swallowed Hemingway*—because these two great men bore witness to the enantiodromiac nature of man's *becoming*.

Literature may not be enough to resolve the human condition, but it does reflect the geography of man's soul; and I *know* now which country a writer is exploring by the stories they write, like the pessimistic novelist Philip Roth who wrote about the geography of *non-being* with such passionate intensity it makes me cringe.

"When the whole world doesn't believe in God, it'll be a great place," he vaunted, with that defiant conceit of the wounded hero, to Rita Braver in her 2010 CBS interview, revealing the meaninglessness and absurdity of life in the country of *non-being*; and like every hapless denizen of this scorched land of lost souls, he will go to his grave blind to the meaning and purpose of his own *being*. But that's life, as seen through the eyes of one of America's greatest writers…

19. *When the Two Become One*

I did *not* imagine my past-life regression to the Body of God where all new souls come from; and I did *not* imagine my regression to my first primordial human lifetime where I experienced the dawning of my reflective self-consciousness; and I did *not* imagine my soul travel experience to the inception of life on planet Earth; but I needed the miraculous power of imagination to connect the dots of my incredible experiences to solve the riddle of the human condition…

In the *Gospel of Thomas*, when someone asked Jesus when the kingdom of heaven would come Jesus replied: *"When the two will be one, and the outer like the inner, and the male with the female neither male nor female."*

This is our transcendent Self, which St. Thomas called "one soul in two bodies with no hypocrisy," and Jesus called *"the peal of great price,"* the individuated consciousness of our soul that I created out of my inner and outer self by "working" on myself with the teachings of the secret way that Gurdjieff awakened me to and which I found in Christ's cryptic sayings and parables.

"Whoever finds the interpretations of these sayings will not taste death," said Jesus in the *Gospel of Thomas*, which by the grace of God I found and lived night and day until I made the two into one, and then I could proudly say: **"I am what I am not, and I am not what I am; I am both, but neither: I am Soul."** That's how I resolved the issue of the human condition and impenetrable riddle of life.

So when I read Jean Paul Sartre and Albert Camus and Philip Roth and Saul Bellow and David Foster Wallace and Martin Amis and Margaret Atwood or any other writer who manifestly reflect the consciousness of *non-being* in their stories, I know where they're coming from; and I admire their courage to tell it as they see it.

It's unfortunate that these writers believe that what they see is the way life is, but it is only one part of the equation of man's enantiodromiac nature; and not until they bridge the great divide of their *being* and *non-being* will they see life as it truly is—a glorious miracle of birthing the consciousness of God with each new "I" of God.

"There is nothing but the self and God," said Jesus; but Philip Roth does not believe in God, or the individual self. He believes our self is a "theatre," a troupe of many players, each strutting and fretting their hour upon the stage and then is heard no more, not unlike the Buddhists who believe that our individual self is illusory and unreal; and as frightening as this perspective may be, the irony is that it is absolutely true. This is the mystery of the soul of man, which both is and is not what it is; and not until we bridge the great divide of our *being* and *non-being* will we resolve the paradoxical nature of our own identity.

Gurdjieff understood this. He also believed that our individual self is made up of hundreds and thousands of little selves, each as ephemeral as the other; and not until we coalesce the "theatre" of our many selves will we be one self. That's the essence of Gurdjieff's teaching, and by "working on oneself" we can take evolution into our own hands and complete what Nature cannot finish.

I *know* from my own incredible experiences that we come into the world as immortal souls, and I *know* that we have to evolve through life to individuate the consciousness of our immortal soul; and it doesn't really matter what Gurdjieff believed about our immortal soul, the reality is that Nature can only evolve us so far in the evolution of our individual self, and not until we take evolution into our own hands will we complete what Nature cannot finish and realize the wholeness and singleness of self that Jesus called *the pearl of great price*; but it took me years to connect the dots and make sense of the paradoxical nature of our *becoming*…

In my teens I had three past-life regression dreams that I still remember as if they happened yesterday. In one past life I was a black slave in southern Georgia, in another I was a North American Indian, and in the third I was a fish monger in London, England; but I never made sense of my past-life dreams until I had seven past-life regressions when Penny and I moved to Georgian Bay.

I had one question going into my regressions that I *had* to answer: why was I so different from my family? I didn't belong in my family, and I believed it had something to do with a past-life relationship; and I got my answer. But I tell all of this in my novel *Cathedral of My Past Lives*, so I need not expound upon it here; suffice to say that I got more answers about my life than I bargained for, and the one answer that helped me resolve the riddle of the human condition had to do with what we bring with us every time we take on a new life.

I had one lifetime in Paris, France in the mid-17th Century that was so sexually and morally debauched that I turned on our Holy Mother Church and Jesus Christ and God, and I died in a rat-infested dungeon under the streets of Paris when I was tried and condemned for "abomination and heresy" (I was known as *"le salaud de Paris)* by a secret tribunal of the Holy Mother Church; and I brought that karmic baggage with me into every new life that I was born into, and which I finally discerned was responsible for my poem *Noman* and the incontrollable sexual experience that brutally shocked my conscience awake and catapulted me into my quest for my true self.

Little do people realize just how much we are influenced by our past lives, but I could no longer deny it when I began to connect the dots of my past lives with my current lifetime; and I went for a spiritual healing with St. Padre Pio because I was finally ready to confront the horror of my archetypal shadow self, which became the basis of my novel *Healing with Padre Pio*.

It finally dawned on me as I connected the dots that the personality that we create with every new life we live stays with us when we die, and we bring this personality with us into our new life; but we are not aware of it because our past life personalities become a part of our personal unconscious and remain hidden. And because every personality that we create has its shadow side, we bring our archetypal shadow self with us also as karmic baggage; this is how the natural process of individuation works through karmic growth and reincarnation.

And so life after life after life, we grow and evolve in our own identity until life can no longer satisfy the longing in our soul to be all that we are driven to be; and that's when all hell breaks loose and we either cry foul and curse the gods, or we look for another way to satisfy the longing in our soul to complete our destiny. And herein lies the mystery of our *becoming*, because we grow in our own identity through the enantiodromiac process of our *being* and *non-being*.

I have to thank Carl Jung for his insight into the enantiodromiac nature of life, a concept that he got from the Greek philosopher Heraclitus; but all enantiodromia means is that everything in life is in a state of flux, always evolving into its opposite: day into night, heat into cold, good into evil, love into hate, and so on; which the existentialist Jean-Paul Sartre philosophized as the *being* and *non-being* of our *becoming* in his dialectical tome *Being and Nothingness*.

But as Sartre concluded, we are what we are not and we are not what we are; we are in a perpetual flux of *becoming*. Hence his conclusion that life was a useless passion, because the logic of his philosophical dialectic could not fathom *the pearl of great price*. But I knew in my gut that there was more to life, which is why I dropped out of university to forge my own path to wholeness and singleness of self.

Like all denizens of the country of lost souls, Sartre could not fathom how to bridge the great divide of his *being* and *non-being* and realize his transcendent Self, and he spent his life philosophizing about the desolate geography of lost souls where God does not exist and man is condemned to be free; a sad and lonely place to be. But I fathomed how to transcend myself, and I was even foretold that I would square the circle and bridge the great divide of my *being* and *non-being* years before it happened while I was studying philosophy at university.

It was my second year of studies and I was in my bedroom reading Ouspenky's book *In Search of the Miraculous*, but I was at my wit's end trying to make sense of Gurdjieff's teaching. I was so disgusted that I threw the book down and just stared blankly into empty space. "What's the point?" I said, and switched the lights off and lay on my bed and stared into the darkness wallowing in despair.

Five, ten, maybe fifteen minutes later a tiny dot of blue light appeared out of the darkness at the foot of my bed and rested suspended in mid-air. I stared and stared, and then to my further astonishment the dot of blue light began to slowly form a circle about three feet in diameter with a big hole in the center. I could not believe my eyes.

I shut my eyes and opened them again, but the perfectly shaped donut of blue light was still there. And then a tiny dot of yellow light appeared at the top of the circle and began to form a straight line inside the circumference, and it stopped, made a ninety degree turn and formed another straight line, and another, and another and joined itself at the top to form a perfect square of yellow light within the circumference of the blue light; and the squared circle of blue and yellow light stood suspended in the air for what seemed like eternity, and then it disappeared and I was staring into empty darkness again.

Nonplussed, I didn't know what to do; so I just sat on my bed staring for the longest time into empty space. Of course, I thought I had just had a spiritual experience; but I didn't know what to make of it. I knew that in philosophy squaring the circle meant doing the impossible, but what did that have to do with me?

Many years later, after I gave birth to my immortal self in my mother's kitchen that fine summer day while she kneaded bread dough on the kitchen table, it finally dawned on me what my unconscious was telling me that desperate and lonely night in my bedroom in my second year at university when I gave up on Gurdjieff's teaching; I was at my wit's end, but my creative unconscious imbued me with the certainty of my own *becoming* with an *actual* vision of the symbolic squaring of the circle, because Gurdjieff's teaching finally opened up to me with my *Royal Dictum*, and I did the impossible and made the two into one. That's how I transcended myself and found *the pearl of great price*.

20. *The Surrendering Heart*

Writers need metaphor to make sense of life, and the more gifted writers think in symbols, which is the highest form of thought writers are capable of, and from symbolic thinking they go straight to visions; which makes fantasy writing the most creative of all the genres—like Tolkien's *Lord of the Rings,* and J.K. Rowling's *Harry Potter and the Philosopher's Stone.* But that's not literature.

Literature is all about the human condition, the *being* and *non-being* of our *becoming*; and trying to make sense of life is what literature is all about—like Martin Amis's new novel *The Zone of Interest* in which he tries to make sense of the Holocaust, the terminal point in the evil of the world.

"To understand the Holocaust is to understand ourselves," said Amis, and if he could "advance our understanding by one centimetre" he would be content with his accomplishment, because the most that literature can do is "shine a light in the darkness of mere being," which in this case means shining a light in the darkness of man's *non-being*—the voracious void of the Archetypal Shadow of man.

My Roman Catholic faith brought me up to believe in the Devil and that evil was real, and it was Carl Jung who freed me from my Christian belief. Not that the Devil and evil do not exist, they certainly do; but not as I was brought up to believe. "If thou hast not seen the devil, look at thine own self," said Rumi.

This is what literature does best: it lets us look at ourselves. And literature needs metaphors to paint a picture of what we are; even literally, as Oscar Wilde's novel *The Picture of Dorian Grey*—one of the best literary metaphors for the evil side of our nature.

We all have an unflattering portrait of ourselves tucked away in the dark recesses of our soul, which Jung called our shadow self; and we will never bridge the great divide of our *being* and *non-being* unless we make a conscious effort to resolve the energy of our dark nature—which literature cannot do for us, because the most that literature can do is shine a light in the dark corners of our soul.

How, then, do we resolve the central issue of the human condition—bridging the great divide of our *being* and *non-being*? And if we do, will the gatekeepers of literature embrace a story that gives us enough understanding to guide our way through the vast continental no-man's land to *the pearl of great price*?

Here's the picture as I've come to see it from my own journey to *the pearl of great price*: we are all immortal beings, sparks of divine consciousness whose purpose in life is to grow and evolve in our own identity until we realize wholeness and singleness of self; and with every new life we live we grow in our own identity a little more until the natural process of karma and reincarnation can do no more to satisfy the longing in our soul for wholeness and singleness of self.

When life can no longer satisfy our *a priori* need to be all that we are meant to be, we panic and frantically grab at all the life we can in a desperate effort to satisfy the longing in our soul, and we despair when life fails to satisfy us. *"When the whole world doesn't believe in God, it'll be a great place,"* cries out one morose chronicler of the human condition, as if it mattered to the universe whether he satisfied the longing in his soul because only he can bridge the great divide of his *being* and *non-being* and make the two into one.

That's man's dilemma, and the central issue of the human condition which literature explores but cannot resolve. The most that literature can do is shine a light on the *being/non-being* and *becoming* stages of the enantiodromiac nature of the human condition. The American novelist Saul Bellow was awarded the Nobel Prize for Literature in 1976 "for the human understanding and subtle analysis of contemporary culture that are combined in his work."

That's what writers do. They reflect the consciousness of their times, but they cannot change their times, as such. The only way to change life through literature, as Katherine Mansfield realized a few months before she died, is to change our attitude about life and write stories with an *enlightened attitude*.

Katherine told her mentor A. R. Orage that she had to be more to write better stories, but literature could not satisfy the longing in her soul to be more; she had to change her attitude about life. So she went to Gurdjieff for help, and he introduced her to the secret way that helped her create the *enlightened attitude* that she was looking for to satisfy her longing to be more so she could write better stories; and several weeks after their talk on literature Orage saw Katherine a few hours before she died, and he found her "still radiant in her new attitude."

Katherine died young, so she never got to write the stories she wanted to write from her *enlightened attitude*; but she revealed to Orage that to realize her new attitude she had to surrender her old attitude about life, which she did without resistance because she was dying of tuberculosis; just as my friend Alice who was dying of cancer had a change of attitude after reading my novel *Healing with Padre Pio*, a change of heart that gained her *the pearl of great price*.

The gifted Mansfield died before she could tell the story of her change of heart about life, and so did my friend Alice; but I did my honest best to honor Alice's story in my tribute at her funeral service, because I knew that Alice would have wanted me to tell the world why she made the choice she did to heal her breast cancer naturally and not with a simple lumpectomy as she was strongly advised to do.

But what was this change of heart that writer Katherine Mansfield and my nurse friend Alice had that awakened them to an *enlightened attitude* about life? What happened to them that they could let go of their old attitude which kept them from satisfying the longing in their soul to be all they longed to be?

It's a long, long journey from there to here; from the *non-being* of our vain and selfish nature to the humble *being* of our true self; and the only way to bridge the great divide to our two selves is by surrendering the one to the other. This is the ONLY key that unlocks the door to the *enlightened attitude* of the secret way.

When I wrote my high school poem *Noman*, I knew that I *was* Noman; but it took many years of transformative suffering to realize that Noman was the shadow self of Everyman, and what possessed me that shameful night was the unresolved karmic energy of my former lives, my own archetypal shadow self. That's why I knew that what possessed me to do what I did was me but not me; and I was impelled by the imperative of my own conscience to find my true self...

21. *Unfinished Novel*

Penny and I were destined to meet. We were together in three past lifetimes that we remember, but it was one past lifetime in particular that sealed our fate in our current life: our lifetime together in Genoa, Italy in the 18th Century.

We were married with three children, but I humiliated my wife on the dance floor with my mistress at Genoa's most important social event of the year. I broke my wife's heart, and I was honor bound to heal her wounded soul; and when we met in our current life, I could not fathom my attraction to her; but it was karmic.

"I didn't choose you," I said to her one day, a year or so into our affair. "I did a spiritual technique to bring love into my life, and I met you."

That was a foolish thing to say, but it was only the first of many. "How do you put up with him," my older brother said to her on the dance floor at my niece's wedding; but Penny loved me, and she replied, "There's nothing to put up with."

But there was. "You're so full of yourself I don't know how you made room in your life for me," she said to me one day, one of many remarks that always cut me down to size; which is why I playfully believe she must have been a Samurai warrior in a past life, because she can lop off my head before I know it.

She may not be an intellectual, but her powers of intuition far exceed the powers of my mind; and I've grown to trust her judgement implicitly. But it was a long road to hoe before I bridged that unholy divide between us…

"But let your communication be, Yea Yea; Nay, nay; for whatsoever is more than these cometh of evil," said Jesus in Matthew's Gospel, and Jesus goes on to reveal the secret of how to bridge the great divide of our *being* and *non-being;* and then he sums up his counsel to the multitude with one of his most powerful and difficult sayings to live by, *"Be ye therefore perfect, even as your*

Father which is in heaven is perfect." And that's how the two are made into one.

Christ's *Yea yea/Nay nay* saying was my entry point into the dialogue that I had with my archetypal Jesus in my novel *Jesus Wears Dockers, The Gospel Conspiracy Story*; but I would never have broken the code of this saying had I not bridged the uneasy karmic divide in my romantic relationship with Penny.

There can be no greater pain in life than the betrayal of love, and I had turned Penny's heart to stone in our lifetime together in Genoa, Italy; but we were bound by karmic imperative to resolve our dishonored love, and I had to win back her heart to undo what I had done, and that made our relationship an unfinished novel.

"Our lives have a narrative structure, like that of novels, and at those moments we call synchronistic this structure is brought to our awareness in a way that has a significant impact on our lives," said Robert H. Hopcke in *There Are No Accidents, Synchronicity and the Stories of Our Lives*; and it was not an accident that I first met Penny in her corner store in my hometown of Nipigon, because she was a bookkeeper and I needed one badly. But it took her weeks to build up the courage to sort out the jumbled papers that I had brought to her in a cardboard box, as though sensing what was to come; and when she finally did our fate was sealed, and we became passionate lovers.

One morning years later in Georgian Bay, I was in the bonus room above the garage of our new home which I had turned into a cozy writing den, Penny quietly entered and asked if she could have coffee with me. "Of course," I said, and stopped writing, making sure to save what I had just written on my computer hard drive.

My morning writing time was sacred to me, which Penny had learned to respect; but our morning chat was so pleasant that she asked again the following morning if she could have her coffee with me, and I could not deny her.

I was working my day job full time, mostly taping and sanding drywall in new houses, and my work was so physically demanding that I had no energy at the end of the day for writing; that's why I took advantage of my morning hours between four o'clock and nine. I was also a runner when Penny came into my life, and running was as sacred to me as writing, and because I had to make a living my contracting business took up most of my time; which put Penny a distant fourth in my obligatory selfish priorities of work, writing, and running.

Work, I had to do to survive, which Penny accepted; but distance running had become central to my spiritual survival. "In running I found my salvation," said "the guru of running," Dr. George Sheehan, whose book *Running and Being* became my bible, and running went a long way to helping me bridge the divide of my inner and outer life. But after eight years of running seven miles after work every day, I burned out on a contract doing seven new houses on the native reserve on the shores of Lake Helen where I went for my daily run, and I had to stop running; but I still had my priority of writing, which took Penny a long time to accept as the driving force of my life that gave me purpose and meaning, and she felt it was a privilege for me to share my sacred writing time with her in our new home in Georgian Bay.

But then one morning she asked if she could have a second cup of coffee with me, which was bold and unexpected; but my reply surprised me even more than it surprised her, because it came from that sacred place of my unselfish nature that I had created by bridging the great divide of my inner and outer self—

"Sweetheart," I said, with the quiet authority of my transcendent Self, "I used to have priorities; but now I have you. Of course you can have another cup of coffee." And from that day on our morning coffee became a sacred ritual; and, my writing never suffered.

The narrative of our life is still unfolding, but we managed to survive the vicious storm that I unleashed with my regression to my past lifetime in Genoa, Italy when Penny was my wife la Donna Francesca and my charming regressionist turned out to be my mistress Gabriella, which became central to my novel *Cathedral of My Past Lives*; and now whenever Penny and I hug in karma-free love, I whisper softly into her ear, playing upon the poet Browning's immortal lines, "Sweetheart, grow old along with me, the best is here already..."

22. *The Endstory*

"The older I get, the more I see that there's something spooky about writing," said Martin Amis in an interview for his new novel *The Zone of Interest*, implying but not quite grasping the mystical nature of the creative unconscious; and though it took some time to realize, Amis also acknowledged that the books he wrote chose him, not he the books he wrote. That's also spooky.

    If the book chooses the writer, which I also happen to believe because all of my books chose me when they were ready to be written, who or what does the choosing? Let's take my novel *Healing with Padre Pio*, for example, which was based upon ten spiritual healing sessions that I had with a gifted psychic; I went for a spiritual healing because, as Padre Pio informed me in one of my sessions, life had brought me to that place of understanding that made me ready for a spiritual healing. The same can be said about writing: life brings the author to the place where they are ready to write the books they are called to write. This is the mystery of writing.

    Every person's story is the same, insomuch that we all have to cross the great divide of our *being* and *non-being*; but how we negotiate our crossing is unique to every person's nature, and this makes every story different. This is so abstruse it's almost impossible to put to words, but having made the journey to *the pearl of great price*, which is the endstory of every person's life, I'm obligated to try.

    I asked Penny one morning what it was about stories that she thought people liked, because I was curious to see how she would articulate why people liked reading stories. Penny has made a habit of reading a few pages every morning as she has coffee with me, and the only book that she could not finish, which was unusual for her because she's adamant about finishing a book once she starts reading it, was Malcolm Gladwell's *What the Dog Saw* that I had suggested because it was "too dry" for her; but not my novel *Tea with Grace*, which she had just fished reading again the morning I asked her what she thought it was about stories that people liked.

She pondered for a moment, and then replied: "You look for the answers to life in the everyday. That's what people look for in stories"—which was the same answer that I got on the road to Midland the day I mused about how to make my point about how stories convey the meaning and purpose of life: **"the guidance and understanding that stories give us."**

But why stories? Why not poetry, which is much more insightful about life than stories will ever be? And why not essays? Essays are discursive, climbing the ladder of dialectical thought all the way to rational clarity; why not essays? And biographies? I like biographies, but like Jung I also don't trust them; so it comes back to stories. What is it about stories that keep readers coming back for more?

"I made things up in order to be able to tell the truth," said Francisco Goldman in *The Paris Review* of his autobiographical novel *Say Her Name*, the story of his great love for his young wife Aura Estrada who was tragically killed in a surfing accident, when he was asked why he wrote a novel instead of a memoir; which my literary mentor Ernest Hemingway had to acknowledge when he tried to tell it as it was without the magic dust of imagination in *Green Hills of Africa*. Which brings us right back to the mystical power of the creative unconscious.

The novelist John Irving does not start a new novel until he gets the first and last sentences of his novel. His first sentence will come to him "out of the blue," and it could be days, weeks, and months before his last sentence offers itself; and then he's ready to sit down and write his novel. If that's not spooky, nothing is!

But it's not spooky for me, because I've grown to trust how the creative unconscious works, which I've come to believe is the same "it" that I call the omniscient guiding force of life that is responsible for all those little coincidences and synchronicities that we experience when we are ready for new guidance and understanding, the same divine agency that flows through all of life that in some traditions is called the *Creative Life Stream* that is the origin of our creation that we call Soul, the same power of imagination that Hemingway called the "dust on a butterfly's wings," and the same ground of all being that Carl Jung acknowledged in *Memories, Dreams, Reflections* after a lifetime of studying the human psyche—"I exist on the foundation of something I do not know. In spite of all uncertainties, I feel a solidity underlying all existence and a continuity in my mode of being"—which, as I've come to realize with my own journey to *the pearl of great price,* is Soul, the unrealized/realized nature of who we are that Jesus summed up with spiritual clarity when he said *"I and my Father are one."*

It's much easier to understand Jesus now when he said *"There is nothing but the self and God,"* because the whole universe was created to give birth to the self so God can unfold in the consciousness of God through the life process; which is why I can no longer suffer teachings that try to short-circuit our journey to *the pearl of great price*—because there are no shortcuts to our Soul Self. We have to complete what Nature cannot finish, and the only way to do that is to make our two selves into one, which is an individual responsibility.

Every person has to cross the great divide of their soul, and in their journey can be found the meaning and purpose of life; that's why people like to read stories, because every story gives us a glimpse into the mystical process of our own *becoming* and excites our sense of knowing. But when stories can no longer satisfy our sense of knowing, as the writer Katherine Mansfield came to see, then one has to find another way to satisfy the longing in their soul for wholeness and completeness; and this is our dilemma.

But as unfair and cruel and meaningless as life can be, it is also kind and fair and meaningful because we just keep coming back until we get it right; and when we sink so low that there is nowhere else to go, the merciful law of life steps in to offer a way out of our dilemma, like when I met Penny in her corner store that day.

I did not know she was the answer to my dilemma, and I would never have fulfilled my destiny until I healed the hurt I had caused her in our past lifetime together in Genoa, Italy; but the omniscient guiding force of life knew, and it pointed me in the right direction to help me on my way, just as "it" knew when my friend Alice's healing journey had brought her to a dead end and she was guided by an inner voice to read my novel *Healing with Padre Pio*, because she was ready to cross the great divide of her soul and find *the pearl of great price*.

That's how life works, and it doesn't matter what we do in life everything that we do contributes to the process of our *becoming*; which was acknowledged by Shakespeare's Hamlet when he said, "for there is nothing either good or bad, but thinking makes it so."

But one has to be in a place of understanding to see this, which brings us right back to the guidance and understanding that stories give us, because they bring us to that point of understanding when life can do no more for us and we have to take evolution into our own hands to complete the story of our journey to *the pearl of great price*, which is my cue to bring my story home…

In *Memories, Dreams, Reflections* Carl Jung quotes Heraclitus, "Everything is flux," from which he coined the term "enantiodromia" that he defined as "the emergence of the unconscious opposite in the course of time." This speaks to the state of our *becoming*, and Jung makes it clear that through the enantiodromiac process of our *becoming* we create our true self out of the *being* and *non-being* of our inner and outer selves: "Thesis is followed by antithesis, and between the two is created a third factor, a lysis which was not perceptible before."

It took Jung many years to break the code of the secret way, and when he did he expressed it in the language of psychology to give it scientific credibility; but when all is said and done, all Jung did was tell the story of how to make one self out of our inner and outer self— the very same process that Jesus refers to in his sayings and parables, and the Alchemists, and Gnostics, and Sufis, and the Taoist teaching and all the sacred traditions of the world—the very same process of individuation that literature vainly tries to unearth with every new story.

So, just how do we create this "third factor," this new Self that Jung called an imperceptible "lysis," out of our *being* and *non-being*, the transcendent Self that I realized when I said "I am both but neither" and called my Soul Self?

It goes without saying now that this "third factor" is *the pearl of great price*, the realized consciousness of our divine nature, and like the oyster that creates its pearl over time by adding new layers of its own essence to the foreign object in its shell, so too must we create our own *pearl* out of the foreign object in our biological shell, the foreign object being our divine essence.

The analogy of the oyster creating a pearl out of its own essence is perfect, and Jesus did not choose the oyster by accident to symbolize the process of individuating the precious *pearl* of our divine Self out of the essential nature of our *being* and *non-being*, but unlike the oyster that completes the process in one lifetime, it takes many lifetimes for Nature to evolve us to the point where life can do no more for us; and then we have to complete what Nature cannot finish by changing our attitude about life from one of taking to one of giving—because that's the ONLY way to create enough essence to realize our own individual *pearl of great price*. Giving back to life is *the* secret way to grow.

As ironic as it may be then, Gurdjieff wasn't wrong to believe that we have to "create" our own immortal soul, because it takes conscious effort to individuate the consciousness of our *being* and *non-being* enough to shift the center of gravity of our self-consciousness from the *becoming* process of our *being* and *non-being* to our transcendent Self, as I did that miraculous day in my mother's kitchen.

Imagine if you will then, three circles one inside the other: an outer circle, which is our outer self; a middle circle, which is our inner self; and an inner circle, which is the seed of our Soul Self—the foreign object in our biological body that comes from the Body of God; and imagine if you will that we grow in all three aspects of our self through the natural process of creating and resolving karma with every experience that we have in life. Like rough-hewed stones in the great tumbler of life, we are tossed and turned and bump and grind into each other from one life to the next until life can hew us no further through the natural process of karma and reincarnation; and to satisfy the longing in our soul to be what we are encoded to become, "perfect as our Father in Heaven," we have to step out of life and go on the hero's journey to complete the process of *becoming* our Soul Self.

That's the story of our journey through life; and the endstory of our *becoming* is the story of completing the final stage of our journey to *the pearl of great price*, which my friend Alice embarked upon four years ago when she decided to heal her breast cancer through diet rather than surgery, an endstory that triumphed through sadness and despair that I simply *had* to honour in my tribute at her service on *December 30, 2014* in Orillia, Ontario, which ironically just happened to be the same charming little community that one of Canada's most beloved storytellers Stephen Leacock made famous with his satirical S*unset Sketches of a Little Town*. But there was nothing satirical about Alice's story, though; if anything, it was unbelievably surreal…

23. *Alice's Unspeakable Secret*

I invited Alice for lunch one Sunday after our spiritual service at the public library in Barrie, and we went to the Georgian Mall. This was a year or so before she learned she had a small tumor in her breast that her doctor strongly advised she have removed with minor surgery, but for personal reasons Alice opted to forego the lumpectomy and heal herself naturally through diet, yoga, creative visualization and other holistic modalities, but always guided by her Spiritual Master and her dreams. We ordered Tai for lunch and found a quiet table.

I liked Alice, and she liked me; a genuine affection that touched each other's soul in true friendship. Alice was single again, having just broken up with a man I'll call Tim who always seemed to have a silly self-conscious grin when we talked and who had peculiar tastes in food, which limited his options considerably; but because their relationship wasn't going where Alice hoped it would, she had to break it off. Alice wanted a man in her life, and Tim feared commitment.

"Can you see yourself with a woman for the rest of your life?" she asked Tim one evening after a carefully prepared dinner, wanting to take the suspense out of their relationship; but the answer she got sent a cold chill up my spine.

"My God," I said, dumbfounded. "He actually said that?"

"Yes," Alice said, with an embarrassed smile.

"I can't believe he would say that to you. What did he think you were, chopped liver? How long had you been seeing each other when you asked him?"

"We were going on our second year."

"And he actually said that?"

"Yes."

I shook my head in disbelief. "And he's a Higher Initiate?"

To Alice's horror, Tim replied: "Maybe, if she's the right woman."

Freudian slip or not, it was a cruel thing to say; and whether he belonged to Alice's spiritual path or not, it no longer mattered. But

Alice had a previous relationship with another self-absorbed idiosyncratic bachelor, a self-employed dreamer and underwater photographer who affected interest in Alice's New Age Religion of the Light and Sound of God just to win her over and move into her home, which he decorated with his photographs of tropical fish and coral reef and undersea flora; but his possessive personality was too much for Alice, and she was alone again with her young teenage son. But when she was diagnosed with breast cancer she also had her older brother living in her basement suite to help him through his trying time, and he helped make her special juices with organic fruit and vegetables and gave her moral support on her holistic healing journey.

I asked her one evening in the first year of her healing journey, whether before or after dinner I don't remember, a dinner that Penny prepared for Alice's special diet, if she felt comfortable in her decision to forego surgery; and Alice was adamant that she was getting guidance from the Inner Master and her dreams and felt in her heart that she had made the right decision to heal herself naturally.

"Alice, miracles come in many forms," I remember saying; but the look that I saw on her face told me to drop the subject.

Being a registered nurse, Alice was aware of the consequences of her decision and monitored the tumor in her breast, and for the longest time there was no apparent growth; but at some point it rapidly metastasized and went well beyond the point of surgery, and Alice had to deal with the frightening reality of her mortality; but we didn't know this when we invited her for dinner one weekend.

Alice was delighted, and looked forward to spending the evening with us; but she called the day before to tell us that she had to cancel. She had worked all week and was low on energy and wanted to rest up over the weekend; but Penny continued to talk with her on the phone for a while, and Alice informed her that they were going to check her lymph nodes and give her a CAT scan, and they were both in tears.

I choked when Penny shared something deeply personal that Alice had shared with her on the phone, because it confirmed what I felt from the very beginning but could not talk about; she told Penny that she wanted to be buried with all of her body parts intact, which clearly spoke to the central issue of Alice's healing journey that I had addressed in my novel *Healing with Padre Pio*.

I had given Alice a copy of my novel the summer before when she and a mutual friend came for dinner one weekend, which Penny could not attend because she got a call informing her that her father was gravely ill and she had to fly up north to be with her family; but Alice never read *Healing with Padre Pio* until the following year when she was strongly compelled to read it.

"PADRE PIO! PADRE PIO!" she shouted one morning as she woke up from a very emotional dream, which was loud enough for her brother to hear and which prompted her to call and ask if she could visit because she had questions about my novel that she had to ask me; and her visit proved to be the first coincidence that was to be followed by two more that spoke to the divine guidance that she was getting on her sacred healing journey through cancer.

When she called I invited her to stay for dinner, which she gratefully accepted; but then she asked if she could bring her friend whom I had met at a spiritual service that Alice had invited her friend to attend in Washago, a small community north of her hometown of Orillia, and I said yes and was looking forward to seeing them both, and that's when the first amazing little coincidence happened.

Just as Alice was about to call her friend to extend my invitation, her phone rang and it was her friend inviting Alice to join her on a one day yoga retreat in Wyevale, which was just five minutes from our home in Georgian Bay, the same day as my dinner invitation. Alice called me back to confirm the invitation, and after their Saturday retreat they showed up at our front door still glowing from the sanctifying grace of the divinely inspired coincidence.

Penny prepared dinner, making sure it was suitable for Alice's special diet, and we had a strangely numinous evening, as though our home was imbued with a special grace (which I suspected to be St. Padre Pio's presence); but when we were alone, Alice asked me about vanity, which was the reason I had gone to the psyche medium who channelled St. Padre Pio for my spiritual healing.

It was obvious from the unspoken element of our conversation all evening that Alice was in a state of mortal fear, and when we were alone and she asked me about vanity I knew she had been brought to that place in her healing journey where she was ready to face her greatest fear in the choice that she had made for her healing journey; but thank God I had the wisdom to not address her fear directly.

"Alice," I said, choosing my words very carefully, "it doesn't matter what path we're on in life, when all is said and done all of life is a journey through vanity to humility. Have you read the last chapter of my novel *Healing with Padre Pio*?

"Not yet; but I'm going to," she said, with the most heart-wrenching look of sadness and relief that told me that she knew that I knew her unspeakable secret.

"My last chapter is called 'The Vanity of All Spiritual Paths,' and it'll give you the answer you're looking for," I said; and before Alice and her friend left that evening I gave them both a copy of my novel *The Golden Seed* and my memoir *The Lion that Swallowed Hemingway,* never expecting in a million years that when her son read to his mother from *The Lion that Swallowed Hemingway* on the day before she died that it would initiate the third coincidence that enlightened Alice's family on the choice she had made to forego surgery for natural healing, leaving them all in a state of wonder from the grace bestowed upon them by the sanctifying power of Alice's choice …

24. *Letter to Alice*

"I've never experienced anything like that in my life," said Alice's friend about our numinously imbued evening. "The moment I stepped into their house, I felt an incredible feeling of love," she said to Alice, and asked her for our email address so she could thank us properly; but that didn't surprise us, because we've had other friends who visit us respond with similar mystified feelings.

One friend in particular who lives in Toronto but has a cottage in Georgian Bay near our home and who's had Christmas dinner with us enough times for it to be called a ritual said, "I just love it here! I don't know why, but I never want to leave when I'm here!" Ironically, this friend also got breast cancer a few years ago; but she followed her doctor's advice and is cancer free today.

And that's the unspeakable secret that compelled Alice to read my novel *Healing with Padre Pio*, because she had been brought to that place of understanding where she was ready to face the terrifying truth of her choice for healing her cancer naturally.

I couldn't get over our evening either, which I knew was blessed with the presence of a higher energy, and all day Sunday I had the strongest feeling to write Alice a letter; but I didn't know exactly what to say. I just had a feeling that I should write to comfort her, because I knew how much she was hurting. And then the theme of my letter came to me, as it always does whenever my Muse wants me to write, and Monday morning I sat down and wrote my letter.

Compassion compelled me to write my letter, because I knew Alice's unspeakable secret; and I had to tell her that she had made the right decision for her healing journey. I knew in my heart that she had made the right decision of diet over surgery, because my journey to *the pearl of great price* had informed me with the sacred knowledge of the secret way that in the Divine Plan of God there are no right and wrong choices; only choices. So every choice we make in life is both right and wrong, and I had to share this with Alice to alleviate the insufferable anguish of her unspeakable secret.

TRUST. That was the issue of her unspeakable secret that Alice had been brought to face by the unbearable distress of her healing journey, a suffering so intense that it transformed the very core of her being; that special kind of suffering that makes the two into one and has been called the slow burning love of God.

Alice trusted the Inner and Outer Master of our spiritual path to heal her cancer, but when it metastasized beyond medical intervention and condemned her to her death she fell into the darkest pit of despair—DOUBT; and she was forced to question her sacred trust in the Inner Master who held her destiny in his hands.

This was the pain that I felt Saturday evening over dinner and after, and I had to write my letter to let her know that she had not misplaced her trust in the Inner Master, because it was a presumption to believe that we know which path is best for us; but how could I possibly convey that sacred knowledge to her? It was beyond me.

I knew what I had to say, but I had to find the right context for Alice to understand the sacred knowledge that had been granted to me by virtue of my own sacred journey of spiritual healing; and for that I had to abandon to my creative unconscious, which I call my Muse.

This is the mystical aspect of writing that all writers experience and call spooky. Norman Mailer even wrote a book called *The Spooky Art: Thoughts on Writing*; but it's not spooky at all if one accepts the divine aspect of their own nature, which for me had long been a foregone conclusion; so I abandoned to my creative unconscious and let the spooky "it" guide me in my letter:

Letter to Alice

Monday, November 10, 2014

Dear Alice, for the past few days I've had a feeling that I should share a thought (concept, idea, or epiphany; I don't know which) with you; something which I know in my heart will give you some measure of relief on your healing journey, and it has to do with what I have come to call life path choices.

A life path choice is a choice that alters our life path. For example, a person may have outgrown their job and decides to go back to school to study law, something they've always wanted to do;

so they quit their job and go back to school and study law and become a lawyer. They've made a life path choice that takes them on a completely new trajectory. This is an obvious example; but there are many cases where life path choices are not so obvious. They are subtle and may take years before we realize that we altered the course of our life with that one decision. But this begs the question: how do we know we have chosen correctly? How can we be certain that when we make a life path choice it is the best choice for us?

Believe it or not, answering this question became the premise of my novel *The Golden Seed* that I gave to you and your friend Saturday evening. This novel was inspired by an experience I had many years ago when I was faced with the quandary of not knowing if the choices I made were right for me.

I couldn't be sure, and so I "let go and let God" by tossing a coin and letting "chance" decide for me. The working title of my novel was "The Flip" before it became *The Golden Seed* many years later when I finished writing it, so I have intimate knowledge of just how difficult it can be to come to terms with the dreaded question: how can we be sure that we have made the right life path choice?

And that, Alice, is why I'm writing you this letter; because you were faced with a life path choice when you were diagnosed with breast cancer, and I know in my heart that you are hurting from the nagging doubt that still lingers from the choice you made.

Please forgive my presumption if I've read you incorrectly, because the last thing I would ever do is add to the pain you must be feeling. On the contrary, I am writing in the hope that what I have to share may relieve some of your unbearable anguish; and I share this only because I was nudged very strongly by my Muse to share it with you. So, if I may; let me share my insight on life path choices…

Since you're acquainted with my writing, you know very well that I'm not one to be boxed in by any particular teaching, including our own spiritual path which I'm sure my novel *Healing with Padre Pio* made abundantly clear to you; and because of my outside-the-box perspective I can offer you a point of view on life path choices that may at first blush disconcert your perfectly normal sense of reason, but upon closer examination may just provide an answer to the dreaded question: how can we be certain that we have made the right life path choice?

I had no idea when I decided to go for a spiritual healing with the gifted psychic who channeled St. Padre Pio that I had made a life path choice; but writing my novel *Healing with Padre Pio* turned out to be a life path choice that has taken me to new spiritual horizons, and my understanding of karma and reincarnation and spiritual growth has been considerably expanded.

Which brings me to the point of my letter: whenever we make a life path choice we set upon a course that will see our life path choice to the end, whatever that end may be; but having made that choice does not negate the life path choice we could have made, because that other choice that we did not make is lived out in another reality!

This is a difficult concept to apprehend, let alone comprehend, and you should take a moment or two to think about it; but if you can't fathom this mystery, let me offer you an explanation that may help you to grasp the concept of parallel lives.

As you know from our spiritual path, Soul just IS; which means that being Soul, we exist in the eternal NOW. There is no timeline for Soul, because Soul just IS. I have no problem with this belief, but I do have a problem with how our spiritual path uses this belief to short-circuit the process of natural growth and evolution to our higher Self by simply saying "We are Soul," because we cannot bypass the entire process of individuating our inner and outer self and making our two selves into one, which is the only way to realize our higher Self. With all due respect to our spiritual path, Alice; the wish alone does not make it happen. We have to grow in the realization that we are Soul, otherwise what would be the purpose of life?

We cannot deny that we have a physical body that gets sick and dies; that's a cold hard fact of life. I know that our higher Self is Soul, and that Soul is eternal; but our body is the vehicle that we have taken on to realize our higher Self. And realizing our higher Self is what the journey through life is all about. And herein lies the problem, which speaks directly to your healing journey; our little human self is always in doubt about what our higher Self has in mind for us.

This was my quandary long ago, which I sought to resolve with the toss of a coin and letting God decide for me; but I've come a long way since those scary days, and I feel that I'm as close to the answer as I will ever be in the realization that our higher Self lives concurrently in parallel worlds with every life path choice that we are faced with!

In other words, the life path choice that you are on now is the life path choice that you have focused your conscious attention on because this is the one your higher Self wants you to be conscious of—for whatever reason; this is between you and God. In other words, Alice; I believe that the choice you made to not go the medical route for your healing journey simply means that this is not the life path choice that your higher Self has focused your attention on, and I believe that the life path choice to go the medical route is being lived concurrently in a parallel world. I know this sounds so outlandish some would call it crazy (but not some quantum physicists and creative writers like Kate Atkinson whose novel *Life after Life* is about her protagonist Ursula Todd living her life in parallel worlds), but I have come to believe that we live every life path choice concurrently in parallel worlds!

Now, if I may be allowed to offer you what I feel about this, given your incredible coincidence with your friend and our Saturday dinner (not to mention that bizarre coincidence of the sign you saw in Home Depot that said TRUST OSTOCCO TOOLS, O being the initial of my first name and STOCCO being my surname, a truly numinous coincidence that I honestly believe the divine law of synchronicity gave to you to help you trust the message of my novel *Healing with Padre Pio*), I would say with total assurance that you have decided to focus your attention on your life path choice of natural healing because this is the path that will maximize the spiritual benefits of your suffering in your sacred journey to humility.

Do you remember what I concluded in *Healing with Padre Pio*, that all of life is a journey through vanity to humility? Well, every life path choice we make takes us down this journey; but some are more difficult than others. And you decided to focus your attention on your natural healing journey to maximize the spiritual benefits of your suffering, which I believe is the Sacred Contract that you made before you came into this world, and my heart goes out to you because I know how difficult your journey through vanity must be. But please, oh please do not ever feel guilty for the choice you made in your healing journey; because in God's world all life path choices are the right path for Soul, and the path you chose will garner you the pearl of great price!

All my love,
Orest

25. *The Holy Fire of God*

I did not email my letter to Alice. As strongly nudged as I was to write it, I was nudged even more strongly to not send it; and I could not understand why. All I knew was that if I sent it I would be interfering in Alice's healing journey, and my respect for the sanctity of individual freedom prevented me from sending it.

But why did I feel so strongly that if I sent it I would be interfering in Alice's sacred journey when I was so strongly nudged to write it? What was the point of my letter if not to give Alice some relief from the unbearable anguish of her unspeakable secret? I could not fathom why, but I had to trust there was a reason; as there always is with everything we do, even if we don't find out until much later…

About three weeks after I wrote Alice my letter, which despite how much I tried to convince myself that I should sent it I just couldn't, I was strongly nudged to drive to Orillia to visit Alice; it was like I heard her calling out to me, especially Sunday morning when I asked Penny if she would like to drive to Orillia.

I had been watching a cooking show on television called *You Gotta Eat Here,* and one show featured a restaurant in Orillia called *Tre Sorelle*, which in Italian means three sisters; and I asked Penny if she would like to try it out.

Penny said yes, and we drove into Orillia; but it was a little too early for dinner, and I told Penny that I wanted to drop in to see how Alice was doing; and when I knocked on her door and Alice answered, the look on her face changed from one of forlorn sadness to joy, and I gave her a long and loving hug.

But there was much more to dropping in on Alice just to see how she was feeling; it went so far beyond compassion that it bordered on divine intervention, because Alice woke up from a dream that very morning that she could not fathom, and I was "summoned" to visit her so I could interpret her dream and remove all doubt about the choice she had made to not have surgery and heal herself naturally, a dream fraught with so much symbolic meaning that it brought tears of joy to my eyes, and Alice's.

In her dream, a beautiful woman with long blond hair extended her hand to Alice and gave her a pearl and gold coin, which Alice gratefully accepted; but as much as she felt that her dream had special meaning, Alice could not fathom the Dream Master's message, and she was struck dumb when I explained her miraculous dream in light of Christ's parable of *the pearl of great price*, because it confirmed her sacred healing journey to her Higher Self—just as Carl Jung's dream confirmed his sacred journey to his transcendent Self just before he died.

"Alice, you got the pearl of great price!" I exclaimed, unable to contain the excitement of her accomplishment. "The pearl is your true self, Alice; and the coin is the price you paid for your true self. My God, what an incredible dream!"

I also knew that Alice's healing journey had come to an end and she would not have much longer to live, but I didn't share that with her; it was enough to see the look on her face when I interpreted her unbelievable dream of being rewarded with the pearl of great price.

Alice thanked me for the interpretation, her sad and happy eyes still marveling at the miraculous timing of our visit, and we had tea and talked a while longer; and then I took Penny out to *Tre Sorelle* for dinner, but unfortunately they were not open on Sundays and we went for Chinese instead...

Was it coincidence that we dropped in on Alice that Sunday afternoon because she needed someone to interpret her dream? How many people did Alice know who would have seen the symbolic meaning of her dream as I did, having just written a spiritual musing called "The Pearl of Great Price" which I posted on my blog October 25, 2014, several weeks before I wrote my letter to Alice? In all humility, I don't believe anyone else could have interpreted Alice's dream that brought resolution to her sacred healing journey through cancer.

We all saw it as an incredible coincidence, but I had my suspicions long before this synchronistic convergence of events that brought resolution to Alice's sacred journey that our life, though free to live as we may choose, is paradoxically choreographed by forces beyond our control, and I was summoned by Divine Imperative to assist Alice in her desperate time of need; and within days I began to see why I was strongly nudged to not send my letter to her, which speaks to the most sacred truth of the secret way that I've had the privilege to be granted—the sacred truth of human suffering, which Jesus confirmed when my hero Carl Gustav Jung brought closure to *The Red Book*—

"What do you bring me, my beautiful guest?" Jung's spiritual guide Philemon asked the shade Jesus in Jung's garden at his house in Kusnacht on the shores of Lake Zurich. "Lamentation and abomination were the gift of the worm. What will you bring us?
"The shade answered, 'I bring you the beauty of suffering. That is what is needed by whoever hosts the worm.'"

Jesus spoke to Alice's unspeakable secret and my outside-the-box perspective on our spiritual path that I could never raise with Alice because of her total trust in the Inner and Outer Master of our spiritual path; but I had long since known that the Inner Master was our Higher Self, which Jung also confirmed in his own incredible journey when he realized that his spiritual guide Philemon was an aspect of himself, and telling Alice would only have done more harm than good because it would have interfered in the holy suffering of her sacred journey through cancer to her true self, *the pearl of great price.*

When her breast cancer metastasized and condemned her to die, her faith was cruelly shattered; and the biggest fight of her life was not to stay alive, but to salvage her faith in her Spiritual Master. That was her unspeakable secret that fueled the Holy Fire of her suffering and raised the spiritual temperature to such a degree that it melded her two selves into one and garnered her *the pearl of great price*, and which was precisely why I was compelled not to send her my letter.

Had I sent my letter to Alice it would have interfered in the alchemical process of her holy suffering, the same holy suffering that I experienced with my *Royal Dictum* and Gurdjieff's teaching and the sayings of Jesus that melded my two selves into one, the same holy suffering that every person experiences to grow in their own identity; but not until one is called to their spiritual destiny will they be put through the scorching flames of the Holy Fire of God as Alice was to burn away the last traces of the abominable worm of vanity and gain the most precious treasure in the world, *the pearl of great price.*

That's why I cried with joy when Alice shared her dream with me: she paid in the coin of her mortal life to shed her precious vanity that forbade her from having surgery, but she gained her true Self; and I knew in my heart that Alice had fulfilled her Sacred Contract.

26. *Honoring Alice's Choice*

I hate going to funerals almost as much as I hate going to weddings, if not more. Don't ask me why, that's much too personal; but I've had to deliver two eulogies in my life because I was asked by the family of the deceased, one for a cousin and friend, and the other for an elder native man I had befriended from whom I learned much about life; but out of love and respect for my friend Alice, I felt honor bound to pay tribute to her life. And I'm glad I did, because I was the only person who spoke on her behalf; which came as a surprise to me given all of her friends and colleagues, a surprise that left me wondering.

Never more anxious in my life, I mustered my courage and read my tribute during the reception after the short service nervously officiated by a female cleric of our spiritual community at the Doolittle Chapel of Carson Funeral Homes in Orillia. I titled my tribute "Honoring Alice's Choice" and wrote the date just for the record, because I knew that it would bring closure to the book that I had been called to write on Christ's most sacred parable, *the pearl of great price*:

A Tribute to Alice

Tuesday, December 30, 2014

Life is a divine mystery. Alice's life was a divine mystery, and I would like to share with you the joy of her divine mystery. I know that we live in a death-denying culture, despite the fact that we see death on television every night, and that we get caught up in the immediacy of our daily struggles and pleasures just to keep from thinking about our own mortality; but the hard fact is that we are all going to die, as Alice did at seven o'clock on the morning of December 24, 2014.

I was in my den working on another book when Alice died. The book I was working on is titled The Pearl of Great Price. Suddenly an inexplicable wave of peace washed over me, and I knew that Alice had just crossed over and was at one with herself. I could not contain the joy I felt for my friend Alice, and I basked in the peace she now felt on the other side. And this brings me to the divine mystery of Alice's life; a mystery that speaks to our very purpose in life; a mystery that honors Alice's choice of healing her cancer.

    I was fortunate to talk to Alice the night before she died. Her son Eddie called to tell me that his mother was in the hospital and wasn't expected to last more than a day or so, and I asked if I could speak with her. He put his mother on the phone, but the moment I heard Alice's voice I broke down and cried. I could not contain myself. I convulsed with emotion and through gushing tears blurted out, "Alice, my heart cries out for you. You made the right choice. Please don't be disappointed—"

    My reaction was instinctive. I only had a few moments to talk with her, and I had to let her know that the choice she made for her healing journey was the right choice. I could not let her cross over without affirming her choice, and I was overjoyed when she told me that she wasn't disappointed; but I could not help myself, and blurted out, "Remember your dream of the pearl and the coin? You got the pearl of great price, Alice. You paid for it with your life, but you made the right choice. *You made the right choice—*"

    Alice was heavily sedated, but she was lucid enough to hear what I felt compelled to say; and she moaned with relief, "Oh, Orest," and her voice faded; and those were the last words we spoke to each other, because the following day when Penny and I visited her in the palliative care ward of the Orillia Soldier's Memorial Hospital, she wasn't conscious. We sat by her for three or four hours, but she never came too; but something beautiful happened that afternoon that speaks to the affirmation of Alice's choice, and the divine mystery of her sacred life...

    I first met Alice about ten years ago at one of our spiritual community worship services. The name escapes me, but we held the service in a basement room in one of the assisted living nursing homes here in Orillia; and after introducing ourselves, I asked Alice what had brought her to the path of the Light and Sound of God.

Alice smiled that sweet smile that spoke more than she was willing to say, and she told me that she was always interested in other teachings; but when she told me about her involvement with the Sufi teaching, I felt an instant connection because I had been a student of the Sufi Path long before my spiritual community had even discovered the Persian mystic whose every poem shouts the secret way inherent to all paths, both secular and spiritual. "*Tell it unveiled, the naked truth! The declaration's better than the secret,*" said the Sufi poet Rumi, which became my personal credo and the bane of my literary life.

As the Sufis like to say, "There are as many ways to God as there are souls of man," a truth that I had arrived at on my own and which was affirmed many years later by the only true hero of my life, Carl Gustav Jung, by what he wrote in *The Red Book*, the chronicle of his quest for his lost soul in the depths of his own unconscious, "This life is the way, the long sought-after way to the unfathomable, which we call divine. There is no other way, all other ways are false paths," declared Jung, with uncompromising honesty.

"*There is nothing but the self and God,*" said Jesus to Glenda Green in her book, *The Keys of Jeshua*; and Ascended Master St. Padre Pio revealed to me that life is a journey of the self. He also told me that life is a journey of discovery and peace, and this was the journey that Alice was on. She was looking for her true self, and her quest had brought her to the ancient teachings of the Way known to the modern world as the Religion of the Light and Sound of God.

I came to this spiritual path by way of a remarkable man called Gurdjieff, whose teaching awakened me to the secret way that Jesus gave to the world in his cryptic sayings and parables, like his most sacred parable *the pearl of great price* that speaks to the divine mystery of Alice's life; but before I reveal the divine mystery of Alice's life, let me say a word or two about spiritual paths.

From Carl Jung I learned about the psychological state of misoneism, which means fear of the unknown, a hatred of change or novelty, as Webster defines the word; and all this means is that whenever the status quo feels threatened by something new and different, people circle their wagons. As disconcerting as this may be to anyone who dares to break away from the status quo, as Alice did with the choice of her spiritual path and courageous decision to heal her cancer holistically instead of having surgery, it's only natural for family, friends, and acquaintances to frown disapproval; but it's hard to believe that in an open society as ours people should still behave this way.

The greatest gift we can have in life is the freedom to choose our own path, and to judge a person for the choice they make defiles the very dignity of man's free spirit; but the irony is that regardless what path we choose—be it that of doctor, carpenter, poet, or whatever religion and off the beaten path we choose to live by, all ways lead to the self because the self is the only path there is.

"There may be intelligences or sparks of divinity in millions, but they are not Souls till they acquire identities, till each one is personally itself," said the poet John Keats in a letter to his brother titled, "The Vale of Soul Making." "How then are Souls to be made? How then are these sparks which are God to have identity given them—so as even to possess a bliss peculiar to each one by individual existence? How but by the medium of a world like this?" said the prescient poet.

Trust the poets to get to the heart of the matter. This is why Carl Jung told Miguel Serrano in his book *C. G. Jung and Herman Hesse, A Record of Two Friendships*, just before Jung died that only a poet could begin to understand the mystery of man's divine nature. "Such is Love, the Mystic Flower of the Soul. This is the center, the Self…" said Jung to Miguel Serrano, confirming what Jesus said to Glenda Green., "Glenda, love is who you are," said Jesus, when he appeared to her to paint his portrait, which she called "The Lamb and the Lion."

We all come from God, "who is our home," said William Wordsworth in his iconic poem "Intimations of Immortality," but not until we acquire our own identity, "a bliss peculiar to each one by individual existence," will we return to the place from whence we came "trailing clouds of glory," because we have to become who we are to realize that we are divine in nature; which brings me back to Christ's parable of *the pearl of great price* and the divine mystery of Alice's sacred journey to her true self that I was privileged to be a part of.

Alice's new spiritual path had brought her to herself, but like an infant child learning how to walk leans upon its parents, Alice leaned heavily upon her Inner Master as she learned to walk on her own spiritual legs; but when her cancer metastasized and could no longer be treated medically, she panicked. Doubt is a monstrous beast, and it will devour the most ardent soul; but Alice was a spiritual warrior, and she cried to her Spiritual Master for help. That's when the merciful law of divine synchronicity came into play in Alice's life, which pulled me deep into the mystery of her sacred journey…

The summer before last our mutual friend and her husband wanted to drive to Georgian Bay to pay us a visit, and I asked our mutual friend to invite Alice along and we could all have dinner at our place, which was arranged; but unexpectedly Penny had to fly up north to Thunder Bay because her eighty-nine year old father had taken a turn for the worse, and she was lucky to talk to him before he passed away. Nonetheless, we had a lovely dinner, and after dinner I gave Alice and our mutual friend a copy of my new novel, *Healing with Padre Pio;* and that was the book that inspired the three remarkable coincidences that pulled me deep into the divine mystery of Alice's sacred journey.

Our mutual friend read *Healing with Padre Pio* that summer and found it fascinating, and she invited Penny and me to her home for a barbeque so she could talk to me about my novel, but Alice didn't start reading *Healing with Padre Pio* until that spring, and only because she was strongly nudged to read it; but before finishing the novel she woke up from a dream one morning shouting, "PADRE PIO! PADRE PIO!"

For those of you who do not know, Padre Pio is a Roman Catholic Saint and Ascended Master. He was a Capuchin monk who suffered the holy wounds of Jesus known as the stigmata for fifty years before crossing over to the other side; and he is known to the world as "The Healing Saint" because so many healing miracles have been attributed to him, to which I can attest because he slew my vanity and healed my wounded soul that became the central theme of my novel *Healing with Padre Pio*.

Alice had to talk with me, so she called and asked if she could come for a visit; and I said, "Of course." But then Alice was nudged to call her close friend and ask if she would like to join her because she had introduced her friend to me at a worship service in Washago;

but by pure coincidence her friend called Alice first to invite her to a one-day yoga retreat in Wyevale, which was only a few minutes from our home in Bluewater, Georgian Bay, and Alice was blown away by the timely coincidence.

We invited Alice and her friend for dinner on Saturday after their retreat in Wyevale, but Penny called Alice first to inquire about her diet restrictions, which Penny graciously allowed for; and we had one of the loveliest evenings of our life, which made such an impression upon Alice's friend that she couldn't get over her experience. But that's the effect our home has on people who visit us; and before they left I gave Alice and her friend a copy of my latest novel *The Golden Seed*, and a copy of my literary memoir *The Lion that Swallowed Hemingway*, which was the book that Eddie read to his mother as she lay dying in the hospital and which inspired the third and final coincidence of the divine mystery of Alice's sacred journey.

Alice had questions that night after dinner that had to be answered, and when we were alone she asked me about vanity. "Alice," I said, with a deep sigh, "life is a journey through vanity to humility; and one day we will all have to deal with the vanity of our life. It's the final lesson on our journey home to God."

Again, Alice smiled that smile that spoke more than she could say, or wanted to say, and I knew that she knew I was referring to the choice of her healing journey; but I had to ask if she had finished reading my novel *Healing with Padre Pio*. She hadn't, and I said that she would know what I meant when she read the final chapter called "The Vanity of All Spiritual Paths."

Alice finished my novel that summer, but for reasons that can only be attributed to the divine mystery of Alice's life, I was strongly nudged one Sunday to drive to Orillia and pay her a visit. It was like I heard a silent cry for help, and I had to visit Alice.

Penny doesn't like to drop in on friends unannounced, so I gave her the excuse that I had seen a show on television called *You Gotta Eat Here* that featured a restaurant in Orillia called *Tre Sorelle*, and I asked if she would like to have dinner there; so we drove to Orillia, but it was too early for dinner and we dropped in on Alice for a visit.

I rang the doorbell, and Alice answered. Her eyes lit up at our surprise visit, but I could see that she was deeply troubled. I put my arms around her and gave her one of my special hugs and whispered softly into her ear, "How are you, Alice?"

"I'm much better now that you're here," she replied with a wane but happy smile, and she invited us upstairs for a cup of tea. And that's when Alice told me about her dream the night before, which was the reason that I was called to pay her a visit; a dream that was much too symbolic for Alice to interpret. And that was the second coincidence that helped me resolve the divine mystery of Alice's sacred journey.

Carl Jung said that dreams are the speech of the soul, and in Alice's dream a beautiful woman with long blond hair held out the palm of her hand to Alice. In her palm she held a beautiful pearl and a gold coin, which she gave to Alice; but Alice couldn't fathom the meaning of her symbolic dream and looked at me with anticipation.

My heart leapt with joy, because I knew that Alice's healing journey had born the divine fruit of all her suffering. *"That's the pearl of great price!"* I exclaimed, with the euphoric joy that always attends one of my epiphanies. "The beautiful woman is your soul, and she gave you the pearl of great price that you paid for with your healing journey. The coin tells me that you paid the price for the greatest pearl of all, your divine self; that's why I had to see you today," and I explained to her what Jesus meant by his most sacred parable…

When the disciples asked Jesus why he spoke to the public in parables, Jesus replied: "Because it is given unto you to know the mysteries of the kingdom of heaven, but to them it is not given." This is why Jesus said, "Many are called, but few are chosen." Alice was called to her healing journey, which made her ready for the kingdom of heaven, and I was pulled into her sacred journey to help her understand the Sacred Contract that she had made with herself before she was born.

In Matthew's Gospel, Matthew tells us that one day Jesus went out of the house and sat by the sea side, and a great multitude gathered; and he went into a ship and sat, and the multitude stood on the shore and listened to Jesus. "And he spake many things unto them in parables," thus revealing the secret way of life in a language suited to their understanding; but later, after Jesus sent the multitude away and returned to the house, the disciples asked him to explain the parables, and Jesus revealed to them the secret of the kingdom of heaven. *"Again,"* said Jesus, *"the kingdom of heaven is like unto a merchant man, seeking goodly pearls. Who, when he had found one pearl of great price, went and sold all that he had, and bought it."*

Jesus spoke in code, and we cannot understand the parable of *the pearl of great price* until we realize like the poet Keats did that our own life is the medium for self-realization; and life after life we grow and individuate the consciousness of our divine nature into a bliss peculiar to our own individual identity through the natural process of karmic evolution until life can do no more for us, which is the premise of the secret way of life. "Nature can only evolve you so far," said Gurdjieff, "and then you have to take evolution into your own hands."

That's why Jesus gave us his teaching. *"He that loveth his life shall lose it; and he that hateth his life in this world shall keep it unto life eternal,"* said Jesus, which the ancient alchemists acknowledged when they said, "Man must finish the work which Nature has left incomplete."

This became the central principle of Jung's psychology of individuation, and the reason that Jesus came into the world to teach us the secret way to our true self, which he called *the pearl of great price*. His mission was to teach us how to transform our little human self and realize our eternal divine self to complete what Nature cannot finish; and that was the sacred four-year journey that Alice embarked upon with her decision to heal her cancer naturally instead of having surgery.

When I sat by her bedside in the hospital holding Alice's hand, I noticed my book *The Lion that Swallowed Hemingway* on her bedside table. Her son read from it while she was in the hospital because it was the last book that his mother was reading. Alice had page markers throughout the book, and in hindsight I regret not visiting her as I was nudged to do the week before she was rushed to the hospital; but Providence has a mind of its own, and I had to go with life as it unfolded before me. However, little did I expect the final coincidence that brought Alice's sacred journey to such graceful closure that it brings tears to my eyes whenever I think of how God spoke to us that day.

Before I relate the third and final coincidence of Alice's sacred journey, I have to say a word or two about my book *The Lion that Swallowed Hemingway*. Alice knew that she was on the final stage of her sacred journey, so why was she reading my book instead of one of the books of our spiritual community? And why did her son read from it while she was in the hospital? My book spoke to her, but what was it telling Alice? That's what the third and final coincidence speaks to…

Curiously enough, a remarkable coincidence inspired my book *The Lion that Swallowed Hemingway* while watching the movie *Hemingway and Gellhorn* on TV over dinner one evening, starring Clive Owen as Ernest Hemingway and Nicole Kidman as his third wife Martha Gellhorn. The movie was all about their tempestuous marriage that ended by Gellhorn walking out on Hemingway, which was a mighty blow to the writer's massive ego because Hemingway always left his women first.

Ernest Hemingway was my high school hero and literary mentor, and I followed his career until the day he took his own life with his favorite shotgun shortly after he got out of the Mayo Clinic where he was treated with electroshock therapy for depression; but as much as I loved his writing, I grew to hate the man whose monstrous ego alienated everyone that came into his life.

I had just finished writing a new book called *The Summoning of Noman* that demanded my return to Carl Jung and his psychology, so I had spent the past year reading heavily all the Jungian literature that I was called upon to read, and something that I instinctively shouted as I watched the movie *Hemingway and Gellhorn* set free the idea for my book *The Lion that Swallowed Hemingway*.

To the surprise of Penny and our dinner guests, who had granted me permission to watch the movie in our adjoining sunroom because Hemingway was my high school hero and literary mentor, I shouted: "That's it! He had to be a miserable S.O.B. to become the great writer that he became!" In one moment of synoptic clarity I saw the reason for Hemingway's conflicted personality, which I could not have done had I not studied Jung's psychology of individuation; and I knew that I had to explore my insight creatively in a new book.

The basic principle of Jung's psychology is that we have two selves, one outer which he called Personality No. 1, and an inner self, which he called Personality No. 2; and Jung spent his life learning and teaching the art of integrating our two selves. And the theme of *The Lion that Swallowed Hemingway* was about how my literary mentor tragically failed to integrate his two selves, while Carl Jung managed to do so, which was confirmed by a dream he had late in his life when he saw high up on a hill a boulder lit by the full sun. Carved into the illuminated boulder were the words: "Take this as a sign of the wholeness you have achieved, and the singleness you have become."

I had to mention this backstory to let you know why Alice was reading *The Lion that Swallowed Hemingway*, because it spoke to her sacred journey that Jesus referred to in the Gnostic Gospel of Thomas: "For when the master himself was asked by someone when his kingdom would come, he said, *'When the two will be one, the outer like the inner, and the male with the female neither male nor female.'*"

This is the divine mystery of life, then; when the two selves are made into one self that Jesus called *the pearl of great price*, and which explains why Eddie read from my book as his mother lay dying in the Soldier's Ward of the Orillia Hospital.

Alice had finally grasped the divine mystery of life as I told the story of my own sacred journey in *The Lion that Swallowed Hemingway*; and to confirm that Alice had made the right choice in her healing journey through cancer, the divine law of synchronicity mercifully choreographed the third and final coincidence to bring Alice's sacred journey to her divine self to holy closure...

Alice's brother, Penny, and I were sitting in the waiting room across the hallway from Alice's room; but it was getting on, and Penny looked at me and I knew it was time to leave. I smiled and nodded assent, and Penny acknowledged with a smile, and we stood up to go and say our last goodbyes to a special friend and fellow companion on life's sacred journey.

The door to Alice's room was partially closed, because Eddie was reading from *The Lion that Swallowed Hemingway* to his sedated mother. Alice's ex-husband was also in the room, as was Alice's sister Cathy, and we stole quietly into the room as Eddie read the last paragraph of Chapter 15, coincidentally titled, "The Call of Soul."

Alice's brother, Penny, and I stood silently and listened while Eddie finished reading. I could not believe what I was hearing, and when he looked up, I smiled and said, "Eddie, would you please read that last paragraph again?"

Coincidences are all about perfect timing. Events come together in one's outer life to give meaning to one's inner life, and we walked into Alice's room at the precise moment when Eddie was reading the final paragraph from "The Call of Soul" that affirmed beyond any shadow of doubt Alice's choice to heal her cancer naturally, which initiated her into the sacred mystery of making the two selves into one and realizing what Jesus called *the pearl of great price*; and I had to have Eddie read that paragraph again so I could explain to his family the meaning of Alice's dream of the beautiful lady with blond hair who gave her the pearl and gold coin, and why she had chosen her healing path through cancer. Eddie read the closing paragraph again:

"So, why are we called then? Jesus said to Glenda Green in her book *Love without End, Jesus Speaks*—the phenomenal story of how Jesus came to Glenda Green so she could paint his portrait, which she called 'The Lamb and the Lion'—that there is only the self and God," and after I wrote *Cathedral of My Past Lives* I understood what Jesus meant, because God grows in the consciousness of God through the evolution of its atoms through life; and with the birth of every new "I" of God in man we are called to our spiritual destiny of realizing our own identity. Or so the story goes…"

I could not believe how that paragraph confirmed Alice's sacred journey to *the pearl of great price*, and choking with tears I explained to Alice's family how that paragraph validated Alice's choice to not have surgery and heal her cancer naturally, and they were thankful for my explanation.

I kissed Alice on the forehead and said my final goodbye, and then I shook hands with Alice's family; but on the way out Alice's sister said to me, "Wasn't that a coincidence that you walked in when Eddie was reading that?"

I laughed. "It certainly was," I said, and Penny and I left the hospital and drove to *Tre Sorelle* for a nice Italian dinner. Penny had veal parmesan and homemade fettuccine and garlic bread, and I had the same but with spaghetti instead.

Life goes on, but we should never forget that life is a divine mystery and that we will all be called one day to our own sacred journey; and I want to thank Alice and her family for letting me share her sacred journey with you today. Goodbye, Alice. You were a very special friend, and I'll see you in my dreams.

27. *Confirmation*

If there was an elephant in the room, which I knew there would be, I chased it out by honoring Alice's choice; and the look that I saw on the face of one of Alice's colleagues told me all that I needed to know.

I caught the look on her face as I read my tribute, and on the way out the door the nurse, about the same age as Alice, dressed in black and very proper, scrunched up her courage and said to me: "You know, as professionals we never judged her."

If I had that moment to live over again, I would say, "If the shoe fits," but I said something much kinder. "I know you wouldn't," I said; but her face betrayed her guilt, and that was the big elephant in the room that no-one dared acknowledge. But what's a writer for, if not to tell the truth? *"Tell it unveiled, the naked truth! The declaration's better than the secret,"* said the mystic poet Rumi.

As much as my tribute honoring Alice's choice sent a chill up the spine of my spiritual community, and probably everyone else as well because it was much too outside the box for their liking, Alice's family appreciated what I had to say, and they thanked me with a look of heartfelt wonder; especially Alice's ex-husband who couldn't wait to share the last and final coincidence of Alice's sacred journey.

It was too good to be true, but it was true; and Thayer had to repeat his story a second time. But I still couldn't believe it, and I had to ask Alice's son and her brother and sister if that's what really happened, and they all confirmed that it did.

When Carson Funeral Homes printed up Alice's memorial card with Alice's picture and bio, they had Alice's picture and bio on the front of the card correctly printed; but on the inside they had printed a different name. They had printed the name PEARL instead of ALICE. The family noticed the mistake and had to have the cards reprinted, and after I read my tribute to Alice Thayer came up to me to share the bizarre coincidence, which I excitedly interpreted for him. Alice's name and picture were on the outside of the memorial card (her outer self) and the name PEARL was on the inside (her inner,

The Pearl of Great Price

divine self), which symbolically confirmed my tribute to Alice that she had won the pearl of great price; but how in God's name could they make such a simple mistake without divine intervention?

Alice's memorial card with the name PEARL on the inside confirmed her sacred journey; and after I read my tribute honoring Alice's choice Thayer made the connection and had to share that final coincidence with me. I was so ecstatic I didn't know what to say; but I told him that I would use that to bring closure to the story I was writing on Christ's most sacred parable. "I still can't believe it, Thayer. This goes way beyond coincidence. It's providential," I said excitedly.

"That's why I had to share it with you," he said, smiling.

"Thank you," I said, gratefully shaking his hand.

Thayer's face glowed, happy in the knowledge that his broken marriage to Alice had been dignified with the final coincidence of Alice's sacred journey. We gave Alice's family a goodbye hug, and to beat the coming snow Penny and I drove to Midland and had dinner at Kelsey's and a long reflective talk to bring personal closure to Alice's sacred, heart-wrenching journey to the pearl of great price.

♥

Afterward

It puzzled me why the merciful law of divine synchronicity would honour my tribute to Alice with that final coincidence of her memorial card, but when I realized that it wasn't *I* that needed convincing of her sacred journey it made perfect sense to me, because that final coincidence was necessary to bring literary closure to the hero's mythic journey that our spiritually famished world desperately needs today; and I got proof of this by way of yet another remarkable coincidence.

The day after I finished writing *The Pearl of Great Price* I was nudged to go on the Internet and listen to one of Dr. Jean Houston's talks; in particular, her talk at Women's Empowerment Initiative at the University of California at Irvine, *December 15, 2013,* and not until I heard what the founder of Mystery School had to say about women around the world empowering *themselves* did I see why I was guided to her talk, which further ennobled Alice's choice—

"…My friends, we find ourselves in the midst of the most massive shift of perspective human kind has ever known. And through it all many feel lost. It feels as if we have lost the intellectual, the psychological, the spiritual, the emotional bearings in space and time, in culture and context. **We seem to lack the cohesive story that could tell us who we are, where we come from, where we're going, and why**…"

This was why I was called to write *The Pearl of Great Price*, and why I was compelled to write my tribute honouring Alice's choice; because not only did my story provide a comprehensive and cohesive narrative for our purpose in life, but with Alice's sacred journey my story provided *actual* proof of another hero's journey. Alice's choice sanctified suffering and gave the human condition the context it needs to make sense of life, and I had to share this final thought with you that whatever choices we make in life, they all serve our highest good on our own interminable journey to *the pearl of great price.*

Orest Stocco,
Georgian Bay, Ontario
February 10, 2015

About the Author

Orest Stocco was born in Calabria, Italy. He immigrated to Canada and studied philosophy at university. A student of Gurdjieff's teaching for many years, his passion for writing inspired such works as *The Lion that Swallowed Hemingway* and *Healing with Padre Pio.* He lives in Georgian Bay, Ontario with his life mate Penny Lynn Cates. His personal dictum is: Life is an individual journey.
Visit him at: http://ostocco.wix.com/ostocco
Spiritual Musings Blog:
http://www.spiritualmusingsbyoreststocco.blogspot.com

ME AND MY SISPHYEAN ROCK